COOKING BY METHODS

Dr. Luis Mispireta

Published in the United States of America

ISBN 979-8-89395-687-0 (SC)
ISBN 979-8-89395-686-3 (Ebook)

Library of Congress Control Number: 2024921997

Mispireta Family Foundation
222 West 6th Street
Suite 400, San Pedro, CA, 90731
www.stellarliterary.com

Ordering Information and Rights Permission:

Quantity sales. Special discounts might be available on quantity purchases by corporations, associations, and others. For details, contact the publisher at the address above.

For Book Rights Adaptation and Other Rights Permission. Call us at toll-free 1-888-945-8513 or send us an email at admin@stellarliterary.com.

Contents

CHAPTER 1

Cooking Methods

COOKING BY METHODS

INTRODUCTION

Cooking is difficult unless you understand the cooking methods.

Cooking occurs when heat is transferred from a source to food products. This energy transfer occurs through air, water, and oils due to the collision of fast-moving or vibrating molecules or particles of these mediums with slower ones. Most cooking methods use all three, although a predominant one is used to segregate the cooking methods in the table. below. Then, we further segregate them by the form of heat transfer.

Conduction is by direct contact between the heat source, a conductor (e.g., a pan), and the food product.

Convection uses the phenomenon of energy absorption by a fluid (liquid or gas/vapor), which causes the heated portion of the fluid to rise and sink as it cools off. In the kitchen, it usually occurs in a closed space like an oven, where the vapor will be the fluid in simmering dishes or air will be the fluid in roasting dishes.

Radiation is the transfer of pure energy that warms the receiving product, like the earth heated by sunlight. Cloud cover blocks the infrared portion of the spectrum (heat) but not the ultraviolet portion, so it is still possible to get a sunburn on a cloudy day without feeling the heat.

Radiation has long been utilized for cooking. A classic example is cooking over an open fire, placing the food product downwind from the fire so the radiated energy, not the open flame, is used for cooking. Modern ways of using radiation of heat include microwaves and infrared grills. *Radiation is the only modality of heat transfer that does not require contact with the heat source.*

Each cooking method has a unique effect on food. We have discussed the impact of heat on each of the macronutrients of the ingredients we may use to prepare our dishes. In general, the ingredients contain all the macronutrients, and they will change with heat; sugars will melt but not evaporate; starches will gelatinize; proteins will denature and agglutinate; fats will melt, and if overheated, they will smoke and change the nature of their fatty acids and form trans fats.

Additional changes occur when food products (ingredients) are subjected to special conditions created by a cooking method. These are the browning reactions of caramelization and the Maillard reactions, a series of reactions between the proteins and amino acids from the proteins breaking down and the sugars present in the ingredient being cooked. Meat, for example, contains proteins and amino acids, carbohydrates in the form of glycogen in the muscle fibers, and fats in the marbling between the muscle fibers and the fat around the muscle itself.

The browning reaction produces flavors, aromas, and appearances that are characteristic of the cooking process and do not enhance or slightly modify the flavor or appearance of the ingredient as seasonings, herbs, and spices do. This browning reaction is non-enzymatic, different from the enzymatic process of spoilage.

The information in the table below describes some easily recognized methods, but others are more obscure. We will briefly explain the less common methods and expand more on the most used methods.

Table 1 Cooking Methods Table (Morh's, 2012)

NATURE OF HEAT TRANSFER	FORM OF HEAT TRANSFER	COOKING METHOD
Dry	Conduction	Dry roasting, hot salt frying, searing
Dry	Convection	Baking, modern roasting, smoking
Dry	Radiation	Grilling, traditional roasting, rotisserie, toasting
Wet	High Heat	Blanching, boiling, maceration, parboiling, shocking

Wet	Low heat	Coddling, poaching, simmering, creaming, slow cooking
Wet	Indirect heat	Bain Marie, sous vide, steaming, double steaming
Fat based	High heat	Blackening, browning, deep frying, reduction, shallow frying, stir-frying, sautéing
Fat based	Low heat	Gentle frying, sweating
Mixed medium		Barbecuing, braising, flambé, fricassee, plank cooking
Device medium		Air frying, microwaving, pressure cooking, pressure frying, thermal cooking
Non-heat		Curing, fermenting, pickling, souring

Cooking Methods – General Recommendations

One important concept is to simplify your methods. There is power in simplicity. Master the basics first, and your cooking will go much more smoothly.

Remember that perfection is the enemy of success, and that can be applied to many areas of life in addition to cooking. If you have a clear purpose for every step you take, you can avoid repeating steps because of errors on Speed attempts. Speed is not achieved by fast movements but by avoiding repeating steps because of errors. Unnecessary or incomplete steps complicate the process with no gain.

Divide the process into segments that are repetitive and easy to master. In surgery, the doctor organizes the work area where he performs the surgery, stops the bleeding (hemostasis), and ties sutures. The cook hones their skills in using a knife, pairing ingredients, and cooking methods. Like the doctor, the cook also organizes the place of work and has all ingredients measured and prepared, a process. like what does the doctor do when checking the instrument table in the operating room?

Practice your craft with passion and a cheerful outlook. Failure in a single step should not ruin the day; correct it and move forward. Early fumbles clear the playing field for excellent finishes.

Now, look at some cooking methods that will serve you well as you prepare your dishes.

CHAPTER 2

Dry Conduction

Dry roasting is when heat is applied to dry foodstuffs without using oil or water as a carrier. (Wikipedia E. , 2024) Unlike other dry heat methods, dry roasting is used with foods such as nuts and seeds. Dry-roasted foods are stirred as they are roasted to ensure even heating. They can be roasted in a sauté pan or a wok. An alternative is to roast them in an air fryer, reducing the temperature by 10% and the time by 20%.

Recipes of Dry Roasting

Dry Roasted Chickpeas

Ingredients for eight servings

- Star ingredient   Chickpeas cooked 2 cups, or two 15 oz cans drained and allowed to dry.

- Fat   Olive oil spray

- Seasoning   Salt ¼ tsp

- Flavorings   ají amarillo powder ½ tsp, ground

cumin ½ tsp, turmeric ¼ tsp, ground
coriander seeds ½ tsp, curry powder
½ tsp, garlic powder ½ tsp

Procedure

1. Preheat the oven to 350°F. Drain the chickpeas in a colander after cooking until they are soft enough for a fork to pierce them but not unduly soft, or use canned chickpeas. Then, place them in a paper towel and allow them to dry sufficiently for an hour or more.

2. Place them on a cooking sheet prepared with parchment paper in a single layer and dry roast for 45-50 minutes. Since not all ovens are calibrated equally, check them often and stir them for even roasting every 10 minutes. They should be golden brown and crunchy in the center.

3. In the meantime, combine the seasoning and flavorings in a bowl. When the chickpeas are done, remove them from the oven and spray them with olive oil on the cooking sheet. Shake the cooking sheet and respray them to ensure the chickpeas are covered with oil. Toss them in the bowl with spices while hot.

4. May prepare them earlier to serve them at room temperature.

Dry Roasted Cashews

Ingredients for eight servings

- Star Ingredient   Raw cashews 2 cups

- Fat   Olive oil spray

- Aromatics   Garlic powder one tsp

  1 tsp of lemon pepper

  Turmeric ¼ tsp

- Seasoning   1 tsp of salt

Procedure:

1. Place the cashews in a large bowl, spray them with olive oil for two seconds, mix them, or shake the bowl and spray again to ensure they are uniformly coated.

2. Sprinkle ½ of the seasonings and aromatics and shake the bowl; sprinkle the second half of the seasonings and shake the bowl again to ensure uniform coverage of the cashews. Spread them on a cooking sheet covered with parchment paper.

3. Roast at 350°F for 10-15 minutes, shaking the tray every 5 minutes to ensure even roasting. When golden, they are done. Remove them and cool them before serving.

4. If using an air fryer, cook at 330°F for 5-7 minutes, shaking the tray halfway.

We roasted Mature Lima Beans with garlic and ají amarillo.

Ingredients for eight servings

- Star Ingredient   Frozen Lima Beans 600g. or cooked and dried lima beans.

- Fat   Olive oil cooking spray

- Aromatics   Onion powder, Garlic powder, Ají amarillo powder 1 tsp   each
- Seasoning   salt and pepper to taste

Procedure:

1. Preheat oven to 375°F.

2. Place the lima beans in a casserole dish, spread them in a single layer, and roast in the oven for 45 minutes. Check them early to see if they are to your liking. I prefer them crispy. They reminded me of the street vendors when I was a kid, selling crispy lima beans by the school entrance.

3. Using an air fryer, use 335°F for 36-38 minutes.

4. Mix the aromatics and seasonings in a large bowl while roasting the lima beans.

5. When the lima beans are done, spray them with olive oil, shake the dish, and respray them, a 2-second spray each time. While still hot, mix the lima beans with the spices and shake the bowl until uniformly coated.

Dry Roasted Broad Beans

Ingredients for eight servings

- Split Broad Beans 250g cooked from cold to boiling, then boil for 7 minutes.

- Olive oil spray

- Kosher salt 1 tbsp

Procedure:

1. Spread the cooked beans on a cookie sheet and roast them for 25-30 minutes in a preheated oven at 350°F until golden.

2. When done, remove from the oven, spray with olive oil for 2 seconds, sprinkle with salt, shake the tray, and spray with oil again.

3. Let them cool to room temperature before serving.

Roasted Broad Beans (Fava)

Cajun Flavored Pecans

Ingredients for 8-10 servings

For seasonings

- Ají amarillo 2 tsp

- Salt Kosher 1 tsp

- Dried basil, dried oregano, dried thyme 1 tsp each.

- Onion powder 1/2 tsp

- Garlic powder ½ tsp

For Pecans

- Pecan halves 4 cups

- Olive oil cooking spray

- Two tsp of above seasoning blend

Procedure:

1. Pre-heat oven at 325°F

2. Spread the pecans on a large baking sheet lined with parchment paper. Spray with olive oil for 3 seconds, shake the pan to turn the pecans, and spray again.

3. Roast in the preheated oven for 15 minutes, stirring the tray every five minutes.

4. Sprinkle the seasoning over the pecans, stir them, and sprinkle some more seasoning. Roast for an additional 15 minutes, continuing to stir every 5 minutes.

5. Cool before serving; may store in an airtight container for up to a month.

Cajun Flavored Roasted Pecans

Candied walnuts
Ingredients for16 servings

- Star Ingredient   4 cups of halved walnuts

- Fat   2 tbsp of ghee or olive oil
  spray.

- Flavorings   Vanilla extract 2 tsp

  Cinnamon ½ tsp

- Seasoning   Salt ½ tsp

- Sweets   3 tbsp Brown stevia or brown sugar.

  1Tbsp Stevia brown and granulated or sugar.

Procedure:

1. Preheat the air fryer to 200°F.

2. Stir the brown and granulated stevia, cinnamon, and salt in a bowl. Stir well to get all walnuts covered.

3. Coat the walnuts with the melted gee or olive oil spray and vanilla in a bowl and stir them to cover all.

4. Stir the walnuts in the flavoring seasoning mix, then place them in the preheated air fryer.

5. Roast the walnuts for 10 minutes.

6. Let them cool to room temperature before serving.

If you wish to make savory walnuts instead of sweet, see these other alternatives:

- Smoky: Sprinkle ½ tsp of smoked paprika (pimentón), a pinch of cumin, and sea salt to taste after coating them with olive oil spray and before air frying them.

- Spicy: sprinkle ½ tsp of ají amarillo powder or mix it with the smoky blend.

- For a different sweet treat, toss the walnuts in a bowl after spraying them with oil, with 2-3 Tbsp of maple syrup and a dusting of ground cinnamon.

Candied Walnuts

Hot salt frying

It is done in a block of salt and heated in an oven. Then, the oil and food products are placed in it, and it goes back to the stove. A similar technique I have seen and tried myself, as an alternative, is using an appropriate-size river stone brought to tableside to fry steaks on. The problem with this technique is that you must keep the stones hot all the time, as they will crack when cooling down. It works for restaurants, but the procedure is too demanding for the occasional home cook who might do it on special occasions.

CHAPTER 3

Method Dry Radiation

Traditional Roasting and Grilling

It is done on an open fire, using radiation from the fire, and it is still used today for the Asado. Argentine Style. A fire is built upwind from the cooking food product, so the food, is in an open environment. The wind will direct the heat to the cooking food, not directly over the fire. If additional heat is needed, the embers of the wood fire could be moved closer to or under the meat or other food product. This allows for better control of the cooking process to obtain the desired result.

Notice the V shape of the grill rods to prevent flare ups.

In traditional roasting, there is more to an art than precise directions to follow. There is no opportunity to cover the product and no dial to regulate the temperature, so experience and diligence rule. Using an instant-read thermometer helps obtain the desired degree of doneness.

Today, the equivalent to traditional roasting is grilling; it facilitates the process by elevating the platform from the ground to waist level so you can stand. Some grills have covers so you can cook the center of the meats at a lower temperature and allow you to position the heat source eccentrically, creating two different zones in the grill.

The fuel for the heat source can be Hardwood, lump charcoal, briquets, or Binchotan Japanese grilling wood; Thaan is a USA product with comparable properties to Binchotan. Each will produce different temperatures and will burn at various times. Lump charcoal and briquets reach about 580°F and burn for 2-3 hours. The Ogatan, made of bamboo, reaches 670°C, the Binchotan (made in Japan) reaches 700°C and will burn for 7-8 hours, and Thaan, like Ogatan, will burn for 5 hours.

Preparing a piece of meat for grilling is as important as cooking.

- The meat cut should be thick enough to allow for the searing and the Maillard reactions to occur (so the steak flavor will be present) without overcooking the center of the steak, particularly if you like it medium rare.

- Look for marbling of the steak, which is fat streaks between the muscle fibers; this will give more flavor to your steak.

- I prefer chewy cuts, so I do not favor tenderloin, which tends to be lean meat. Many cuts will give you plenty of flavor and value. On the more expensive side, you have the ribeye, the strip, and the T bone/porterhouse (which has a piece of tenderloin and a strip). In the lesser expensive side, you have the hanger or Butcher steak, the skirt (fajitas), Short Ribs, are the lower ribs (asado de tira in Argentina, or Kalbi in Korean), the Flap or Sirloin tip, the Flank steak or vacío in Argentina, the Picaña or sirloin cap or culotte, and the Tri-Tip from the bottom sirloin. All of them are perfect for grilling, are thick enough, are chewy, and have vibrant flavors.

- The source of heat is essential in grilling any product. When grilling meats, you want to sear the surfaces to get the Maillard reactions and the meat flavor from them and cook the center to the doneness you prefer, less cooked than the surface. You need two sectors in your grill, one at a hot temperature and the other at a lower temperature, so your seared surface will not charr. You achieve this by asymmetrically placing the wood or charcoal to one side; the other will get heat from radiation and need longer to get the desired effect without charring the surface.

- There is still the matter of marinades and rubs; each one has a preference or a family recipe. Usually, they have oil, flavorings, salt, and often acids in the form of lime juice and vinegar. The acids will degrade the protein of the meat and, if left too long, will make the meat mushy. If the marinade tastes acidic, marinating in it longer than 2 hours is not a good idea. Concerning the salt, it is best to do it early, for several hours, as salt will penetrate and enhance the meat flavor. The other ingredients of the marinade are primarily surface agents and do not penetrate unless the tenderizing effect of the acids breaks down the tissues.

- An agent that enhances the Maillard reaction shortens the time necessary for the searing. This can be beneficial in thinner cuts so the center is not overcooked. Mayonnaise is this agent. It is a suitable carrier for flavorings and is easily applied.

- There are multiple variables in grilling. The amount of heat produced depends on the quality of the wood or charcoal used, the type and thickness of the meat, and the quality of the coverage when cooking in the temperate zone of the grill. Therefore, the time varies with any change of these variables; one should go by the changes in the meat, visual changes as the crust forms during the searing phase, and internal temperature during the cooking on the temperate side.

- The desired internal temperature varies with the type of meat. For beef, 125-135°F for medium rare, 150°F for medium.

Recipes for Traditional Roasting and Grilling

Roasted Picaña (Sirloin cap)

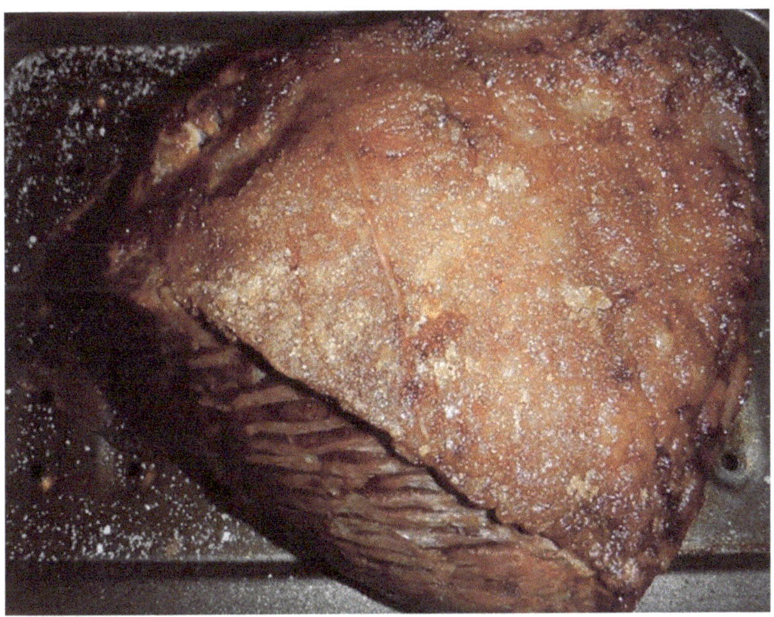

Traditional Roasted Picaña

Ingredients for 8-10 servings

- Protein   Picaña whole (Sirloin cap or Coulotte) 3-3 ½ lb. Do not trim the fat cup. Favor abundant marbleized meats.
- Seasonings   Salt and pepper are applied early, at least two hrs. before cooking.
- Flavorings: No need for any; the dripping fat from the cap will give enough flavor.

Procedure:

1. Make diagonal crossing shallow cuts on the fatty cup.

2. Heat the grill to a hot setting, with a second compartment with moderate heat (set up the grill with an asymmetric heat source - wood embers or charcoal to one side.

3. When the meat temperature is not cold, and the salt and pepper are applied earlier, place the joint fat side down to sear on the hot side (3-4 minutes). Turn it over and sear the meat side for 3-4 minutes. If feasible, do the same on the thick border.

4. Move the roast to the cooler side of your grill, cover it, and roast it to an internal temperature of 130°F (20-40 minutes). The time will depend on how hot your hot side is, so check the internal temperature often to the center of the thickest side of the roast.

5. Remove from the grill, cover with aluminum foil, and stand for 15 minutes.

6. A mushroom sauce will give an excellent finish.

Other cuts

Flank Steak

Treated the same way as Picaña and cooked with the same principles.

Flank Steak grilled.

Beef Steak Shio Koji

Ingredients for two servings

- Two servings of flank beef steak with the most extended expiration date.

- Ten percent by weight of Shio Koji, 1 Tbsp = 20g.

Sauce for steak optional

- Butter 2 Tbsp

- Garlic 1 clove

- Soy sauce few drops.

Procedure:

1. Lightly score the steak.

2. Place the steak covered in Shio Koji in a zip plastic bag, Marinate, and refrigerate overnight.

3. Rest the steak at room temperature for at least 15 minutes. Wipe out the Shio Koji with paper towels.

4. Grill or sauté in a non-stick pan with oil spray.

5. It may be accompanied by fried cauliflower rice or white rice, pilaf style.

For Optional Sauce

1. Add the butter and pressed garlic to a saucepan. Melt the butter and cook until the garlic is golden brown. Turn off the heat and add 5-6 drops of soy sauce.

2. Spoon the sauce over the steak.

Grilled Marinated Flank Steak.

Ingredients for four servings

Marinade

- Worcestershire sauce 4 Tbsp

- Chopped and pressed anchovy filets 3

- Soy sauce 1 tsp

- Sugar 1 tsp

- Garlic 2 cloves pressed or grated.

- Dijon mustard 2 tsp

- E.V., olive oil 2 Tbsp

Shake it well, creating an emulsion. Save one and a half Tbsp for use as a sauce.

Ingredients for the meat:

- One flank steak of about 1-1.5 lbs.

Procedure:

1. Marinate the steak overnight or up to 24 hrs. (The marinade has no acid, no worries)

2. Before starting your grill, clean the grid, removing any residue from previous use. Half an onion in a long grilling fork makes this easy.

3. Bring the steak to room temperature for 30 minutes to an hour.

4. Set up your grill for two hot zones with all the charcoal and a temperate zone with no charcoal. Have a means to cover the steak in the cooler zone.

5. Sear the meat on the hot side, then move the steak to the temperate side, cover it, and cook it to 125°F for medium-rare.

6. Let the meat stand, covered with foil, for 10 minutes before slicing it.

Flank Steak with Asian Marinade.

Ingredients for four servings:

- Protein   Flank steak 1.25- 1.5 lbs.

- Marinade

> Palm sugar or Brown sugar ½ cup.
> Water ¼ cu
>
> Fish sauce 3 Tbsp
>
> lime juice ¼ cup
>
> Garlic 2 cloves pressed.
> Ají Amarillo paste 1 tsp
> Veg. oil ¼ cup

Procedure:

1. In a saucepan, heat the water and sugar to dissolve; after dissolving, add the fish sauce, lime juice, garlic, and ají amarillo, and stir to mix. Reserve half of the mixture and add oil to the other half. Place the marinade in a large resealable plastic bag with the steak. Marinate is refrigerated for 2-3 hours, but it is no longer because of the acid in the marinade.

2. Set up your grill with two zones: a hot one with all the charcoal under this side; the other zone, a temperate one, will have no charcoal under. Light up the charcoal.

3. Remove the steak from the marinade and discard the marinade. Dry the steak with paper towels. Place the steak on the hot side and sear well all surfaces of the steak.

4. Once finished with the searing, place the steak on the temperate side, close the hood of the grill, and cook to 125°F internal temperature for medium rare (20-40 minutes) and 135°F for medium (5-7 minutes longer)

5. Check the internal temperature frequently since the grill's temperature will vary between grills.

Grilled Eggplant Steaks with Gremolata and Tomatoes

Ingredients for three servings:

- Star ingredient   Eggplants medium 2, sliced lengthwise ½ inch thick.

- Fat olive oil 2 Tbsp

- Crumbled farmer's cheese or goat cheese.

- Seasoning   Salt and Pepper to taste
- Aromatics   Grape tomatoes 1 pint.
- Garnishes   Gremolata is a condiment of finely minced parsley, garlic, and lemon zest. (*Gremolata*).

Procedure:

1. Pre-heat the Grill in two zones.

2. Salt both sides of the eggplant slices, rest for 15 minutes, rinse with cold tap water, and tap them dry. Brush both sides with olive oil and grill them for 4 minutes on each side in the intermediate area between both zones.

3. Stack and wrap them in aluminum foil to allow them to cook through and become translucent.

4. In the meantime, make the gremolata. Half the tomatoes and toss them with some salt and a slight drizzle of olive oil extra virgin.

5. On the serving plates, lay the eggplant slices, top with gremolata and then the tomatoes, and you may add crumbled farmer's cheese or goat cheese.

6. You may serve them with lentil salad with onion slices, cauliflower rice, or quinoa salad.

Grilled Flat Iron Steak

Ingredients for 4-6 servings.

For the Marinade:

- Condiments

  Soy sauce ½ cup
  Sherry ½ cup
  Honey ¼ cup
  Sesame seed oil 2 Tbsp
  Ginger grated 2 Tbsp
  Garlic pressed 2 Tbsp
  Ají amarillo 1 Tbsp

- Protein

  2 Flat Iron steaks

- Garnish

  Green onions, two stalks cut in diagonal.

  Sesame seeds 2 Tbsp

Procedure:

1. Mix all the condiments in a small bowl until well mixed.

2. Place the steaks and marinade in a sealable plastic bag, squeeze all the air out of the bag, and refrigerate for several hours; since the marinade does not contain acid, it will not denature the proteins.

3. Set the grill in a 2-zone (asymmetrical positioning of the charcoal) and sear the steaks on both sides until a nice crust has developed. It is OK to turn them several times. Measure the internal temperature; if it is 130°F, it is medium rare. If it is lower, place the steak on the temperate side and cook, checking the internal temperature often. When done, rest the steak for 5-10 minutes.

4. Sprinkle the steaks with the green onions and sesame seeds.

Flat Iron Steak with Red Wine Sauce.

Ingredients for six servings.

For the sauce

- Condiments   Onion 1 cubed small.

  Garlic pressed 1 Tbsp

  Oregano dried 1 tsp

  Tomato paste ¼ cup.

  Ají Amarillo paste 1 tsp

- Fat   Olive oil Light 3 Tbsp

  Butter unsalted 6 Tbsp

- Seasoning   Kosher salt and freshly

  ground

  Black Pepper to taste.

- Wine   Red wine dry 2 ½ cups.

Protein   2 Flat Iron steaks

Procedure:

1. Set up the Grill with a two-zone hot and temperate. As discussed in the general comments about grilling, cook the meat (seasoned and oiled with olive oil). Measure the internal temperature for the degree of doneness. Rest the meat after removing it from the grill and tent it with aluminum foil.

2. Sauté the onions until translucent in two tablespoons of butter, seasoning with salt to taste, about 4-5 minutes. Add the garlic and oregano as soon as fragrant, 30 seconds or so. Stir in the tomato paste and cook while stirring for a few minutes. Add the wine and continue to stir, simmering to reduce it by ½.

3. Strain the sauce and discard the solids. Return it to the saucepan and bring it to a slow simmer, adding the remaining butter in small chunks and whisking the sauce. Season the sauce with salt and pepper.

4. Slice the meat across the grain, divide it among serving plates, drizzle the sauce, and serve. Add slices of shitake mushrooms to the sauce when cooking until soft.

Grilled Garlic-herb Rubbed Hanger Steak

Ingredients for four servings

- Protein   Hanger steak 2lb.

- Fat   Olive oil 2 Tbsp
- Aromatics   Peppercorns 2 Tbsp

  Garlic 4 cloves pressed.

  Parsley 4 large sprigs chopped.

  Shallot 1 large sliced
- Seasoning   Salt kosher 1 Tbsp

Procedure:

1. Rub the meat with the olive oil.

2. Mix the aromatics and seasoning in a food processor until smooth.

3. Rub the mixture on the meat all over.

4. Place the rubbed meat in a plastic resealable bag. Refrigerate for 2 hours or more (no acid in the rub).

5. Cook on a hot grill, turning frequently to an internal temperature of 125°F for medium rare and 130°F for medium. Do not overcook the meat, or it will become grainy and rubbery.

Creole onion sauce:

- Red Onion 1 medium sliced thin

- Ají amarillo paste 1 tsp

- Olive oil extra virgin 2 Tbsp

- Sherry vinegar 1 Tbsp

Mix all ingredients and rest for at least 1 hour to blend flavors. Gets better with time.

CHAPTER 4

Method Dry Conduction, Radiation

Broiling

Broiling is the current version of roasting over an open fire or hot coals (traditional roasting). Broiling uses radiation as the principal mode of heat transfer. All the sources of heat for broiling emit visible light, so they are radiators of infrared radiation. The location of the source of heat is above the food product, and the distance from the food to the source determines how deep the cooking process will go. This cannot be easy, and practice will be necessary. The energy radiated from a broiler is 70-80 times as much as an oven in baking mode. This allows a fast surface browning or caramelization (Crème Brule), while the center may remain cold. For this reason, broiling is an excellent finishing technique for meats for a home cook. Still, they may need a different method for cooking the center, like roasting, sous vide, or grilling on the moderate temperature side of the two-zone setup of the grill.

The following recipe is an example where broiling is the only cooking method used.

Recipes for Broiling dishes

Broiled Parmesan Scallops

Broiled Parmesan Scallops

Ingredients for six servings, each four scallops

- Star Ingredient or protein — two dozen sea scallops
- Fat — Butter unsalted 100g or 7.6 Tbsp

  Parmesan Cheese shredded 1 cup.
- Seasoning — Salt and Pepper to taste
- Flavorings — Juice of 2 limes, fresh

  Worcestershire sauce 1 tsp
- Garnishes — Parsley chopped 1 Tbsp

Procedure:

1. Clean the scallops and remove the side muscle. Pre-heat the oven to broil high, placing the upper oven rack at least 4-6 inches from the heat source.

2. Place one scallop per scallop shell and sprinkle with lime juice and a few drops of Worcestershire sauce.

3. Season with salt and pepper and place some parsley on top.

4. Top with small pieces of butter, cover with abundant parmesan cheese, and crown with a piece of butter.

5. Place them on a rimmed baking sheet. Place the sheet in the oven and broil for 2-3 minutes. They are ready when the cheese has melted and is golden in color.

Note: It is best to grate the cheese from a block; pre-grated cheeses have an anticaking agent that makes the melting uneven.

Carob Cream Brûlée

Carob cream Brûlée

Ingredients for four servings

- Protein   egg yolks 5
- Fat   Heavy cream 2 cups
- Carbs   Carob syrup 3 Tbsp

                        Stevia granulated ¼ cup.

                        Sugar 8 tsp

- Flavorings   1 tsp of vanilla

Procedure:

1. Preheat the oven to 300°F. Heat water in a kettle.

2. In a saucepan, heat the cream with the carob syrup. Do not let it boil.

3. Meanwhile, beat ¼ cups stevia, egg yolks, and vanilla using a wire whisk or a spatula until pale and thick. Add the hot cream in a thin stream, stirring all the time. Strain.

4. Place small ramekins in a large pan with an inch or so of hot water. Bake for 35 minutes in this hot water bath. They are ready when set but quiver slightly in the center when shaken. The water bath should not boil at any moment; if this happens, add more tepid water to the baking pan.

5. Remove the ramekin from the oven and cool it to room temperature. Transfer it to the refrigerator and cool it completely. Before serving, sprinkle each ramekin with a generous amount of sugar (about two teaspoons), and

using a blowtorch (or under the broiler), melt the sugar until golden. If using the broiler, put it back in the fridge until cold.

Clams a La Mar

Clams a La Mar

Ingredients for two servings

- Clams   Top neck or middle neck six clams

- Flavoring   Nori sheets 6

                          Baby spinach leaves 1 cup.

                          Basil leaves 1 cup.

- Fat   unsalted butter 4 Tbsp

- Aromatics   Garlic minced 1 Tbsp

                          Ají Amarillo paste 1 tsp

- Liquid   Dashi ½ cup

                          Lime juice ½ cup

Procedure:

1. Soak Nori sheets in the dashi and lime juice.

2. In a hot pan, sauté garlic and Ají Amarillo until caramelized—Deglaze with the soaked nori and their liquid.

3. Add the spinach and Basil leaves and cook until soft. Squeeze the excess liquid through the cheesecloth. While hot, place it in a food processor, add the butter, and mix well.

4. Top each clam in the ½ shell with the mixture, broil on high for 2-3 minutes, and serve immediately.

Broiled Miso Salmon

Ingredients for four servings:

- Protein   Salmon filets with skin 1-1 ½ lb.

- Carbohydrates   Sugar, maple syrup, or Stevia granulated   2 Tbsp

- Condiments   Light or Yellow Miso 2Tbsp

  Soy sauce Tamari 2Tbsp

  Rice Vinegar 1 Tbsp

  Ají Amarillo paste

- Seasoning   Salt kosher ¼ tsp

  Pepper black to taste ½ tsp

- Garnish   Green sliced onions and sesame seeds.

Procedure:

1. Rest salmon at room temperature for 15 minutes.

2. To make the Miso glaze, mix the seasonings, condiments, and sweet carbs in a small bowl until smooth.

3. Preheat the broiler to high, with the rack at the second-highest position. Prepare a cooking-edged sheet with aluminum foil or silicone silpat brushed with olive oil.

4. Dry each salmon filet with paper towels, place them on the prepared cooking sheet, and liberally brush the fillets with the miso glaze.

5. Broil to an internal temperature of 125°F, 4-5 minutes for thin fillets and 7-10 minutes for 1 inch or more thick fillets.

6. Brush with more of the glaze and serve.

7. It may be accompanied by fried cauliflower rice or a salad.

London Broil

The term London Broil represents more of a cooking method than a specific beef cut. The meat used for London Broil can be from cuts, such as a flank steak, top-round steak, or cuts from sirloin. They are marketed as London Broil, a steak of about ½ an inch to up to 4 inches; the common denominator is a lean and challenging piece of meat that will benefit from some marinade if in the range of ¾ of an inch to 1 ½ inch thick can then be cooked in the broiler, to get a quick Maillard reaction and the center of the steak be at a medium rare and not need any further cooking.

Ingredients for 4-6 servings.

- 1 Beef top round steak, cut 1 to 1 ½ inch thick.

- Acid   Lime Juice ½ cup

- Aromatics   Green Onions minced 3Tbsp

  Fresh ginger grated 1 Tbsp

  Garlic pressed 1 Tbsp

- Seasoning   Salt kosher ½ tsp

- Liquids   Vegetable oil 1 Tbsp

  Water 3 Tbsp

Procedure:

1. In a blender, liquefy all ingredients.

2. Place the mixture in a resealable plastic bag, add the beef steak, and marinate refrigerated for 2 hours to prevent the steak from denaturing from the acid from lime juice. Discard the marinade.

3. Remove the steak and rest at room temperature for at least ½ hour.

4. In the meantime, set up your broiler rack so the meat is 4-6 inches from the heat source and set the broiler temperature to high.

5. Broil the steak for 5-7 minutes according to the preferred searing degree. Turn over the steak and broil for another 5 minutes or so.

6. Check the internal temperature at the center of the thicker portion. It should be 125-130°F for medium rare. If it is below that, lower the heat to broil low and bring the internal temperature to the desired degree of doneness.

7. Rest the meat for 10 minutes before slicing.

CHAPTER 5

Dry convection

Baking and Roasting

Baking and roasting involve the food surrounded by a hot box. This method depends on radiation from the hot walls of the oven and the convection of the air contained in the box. The air heats and rises, then cools and sinks since the heat source is at the bottom. Typically, temperatures obtainable with this technique are in the range of 300-500°F (150-260°C). In today's lexicon, we talk about baking when referring to cakes, pastries, etc., and roasting for savory dishes.

General guidelines for roasting:

- Select tender cuts of meat, such as meat from the ribs or loin areas, tender cuts from the legs, e.g., top round, some tender birds, or fish, e.g., whole chickens or whole fish.

- When cooking vegetables whole, score their skins, to permit the steam from the cooking interior to escape.

- Retain a layer of fat or poultry skin for basting naturally as it cooks. To avoid animal fat, use an encrusting alternative to the skin (egg wash, flour, breadcrumbs, panko, or ground nuts) to prevent the product from drying.

- If you add vegetables or mirepoix to your roast, make the cuts proportional to the roasting time. It will vary with the weight of roasting or size of the roast. If you are adding towards the end of the roasting, cut the vegetables small so they will be fully cooked and caramelized at serving time.

Recipes for Conventional Modern Roasting

Conventional Modern Roasting is done in an oven. It is best to sear the meat before roasting, usually in a frying pan with oil, to create a crust produced by the Maillard reactions.

There is no single cut for Roast beef; the most common cuts used are Top Round Roast, Top sirloin roast, Bottom round roast, Eye of Round Roast, Sirloin Cap, or picaña. Cook them best to medium rare and not more than medium. They are lean and tough meat. If you do not eat any meat less than well done, you should stick to tender cuts, like eye rib, porterhouse, strip, or tenderloin, which can tolerate better cooking to that degree.

Sometimes, you may use the reverse searing technique: the roasting is done first, and when the food is cooked to the desired degree of doneness, the searing is performed.

At times, when roasting a large joint with an irregular shape and the searing in a pan is impractical, it can be accomplished using a torch or starting the roasting as recommended by Lena Abraham from Delish US (*Abraham*, 2023) at a hot temperature for 15 minutes or so and then decreasing the heat to a lower temperature. For example, start at 450°F for 15 minutes and then lower the heat to 325°F until done with an internal temperature of 135°F for medium rare and 145°F for medium. I give 15 minutes per pound, start checking internal temperature often after that time, and remove at the temperature for desired doneness. Remember, after resting, the roast temperature will increase and meet the recommendations for safe internal temperatures.

All the cuts in the recipes for traditional roasting and grilling can be oven-roasted, usually searing first and then roasting after. The most common temperature setting utilized is 375°F, and the roasting time will vary depending on the weight of the meat.

To simplify guesswork, you may use the following table.

(Cattlemen's Beef Board and Cattlemen's Beef Association, 2019)

Table of Roasting times.

TRIMMED TENDERLOIN ROAST

# OF Servings	Weight	Oven temp °F	Doneness	Cooking Time	Remove from oven @ °F
4-6	1-2 lb.	425°F	Medium-Rare	30-40 minutes	135°F
			Medium	35-45 minutes	145°F
8-10	2-3 lb.	425°F	Medium rare	35-45 minutes	135°F

			Medium	45-50 minutes	145°F

Ribeye Roast (Boneless)

# Of Servings	Weight	Oven Temp °F	Doneness	Cooking Time	Remove from oven @ °F
12-16	3-4 LB.	350°f	Medium rare	1H-30 minutes	135°F
			Medium	1 hr. 45min-2 hr.	145°F

Ribeye Roast (Bone In)

# of Servings	# of Ribs	Weight	Oven Temp °F	Doneness	Cooking time	Remove when
4-6	2	4-6 lb.	350°F	Medium rare	1hr 45 min.-2hr-2hr 15 min.	135°F
				Medium	2hr-15 min to 2hr. 45 min	145°F
8-10 Servings	4-5	8-10	350°F	Medium rare	2hr 30 min to 3 hrs.	135°F

				Medium	3 hrs to 3 hrs. 30 min.	145°F

The USDA has issued guidelines for **safe internal temperatures of meats**. These temperatures are for after-resting, not for removal from the oven.

Table 3 Safe Internal Temperatures

Safe Internal Temperatures recommended by USDA. (USDA, 2023)

Product	Minimum Internal Temperature & Rest Time
Beef, Pork, Veal & Lamb Steaks, chops, roasts	145 °F (62.8 °C) and allow to rest for at least 3 minutes
Ground Meats	160 °F (71.1 °C)
Ground Poultry	165 °F
Ham, fresh or smoked (uncooked)	145 °F (62.8 °C) and allow to rest for at least 3 minutes
Fully Cooked Ham (to reheat)	Reheat cooked hams packaged in USDA-inspected plants to 140 °F (60 °C) and all others to 165 °F (73.9 °C).
All Poultry (breasts, whole bird, legs, thighs, wings, ground poultry, giblets, and stuffing)	165 °F (73.9 °C)

Product	Minimum Internal Temperature & Rest Time
Eggs	160 °F (71.1 °C)
Fish & Shellfish	145 °F (62.8 °C)
Leftovers	165 °F (73.9 °C)
Casseroles	165 °F (73.9 °C)

Roasting Vegetables

Also, you may roast vegetables; the ways to improve the results are:

- Do not overcrowd the cooking tray where you place them.

- Put them to roast. Considering the time it takes to roast them, place vegetables in the same tray, which takes about the same time to roast. If space is left in the tray, you may add vegetables with shorter roasting times accordingly. Otherwise, prepare a second tray to be placed in the oven at an appropriate time.

- If you have trays at different heights, use convection roasting if your oven has it. Otherwise, rotate the trays about halfway.

- Do not add oil or other flavorings, such as garlic, onion powder, soy sauce, or Balsamic vinegar reductions, at the beginning. Add them after roasting so the vegetables will not become soggy. Salt and pepper will adhere better after brushing them with oil first.

- Roasting times for some vegetables are as follows, Asparagus 8-10 minutes at 400°F., Brussel sprouts 20-30 minutes at 400°F, Broccoli 16–20 minutes at 425°F, Cabbage 40 minutes at 400°F., Carrots 25-30 minutes at 425°F., Eggplant 15 minutes at 425°F., Green Beans 20-25 minutes at 400°F., Mushrooms (Portobella) 20-25 minutes at 475°F., Peppers 20-25 minutes at 475°F., Spinach 8 minutes at 325°F., Zucchini 5-7 minutes at 450°F.

- Cauliflowers can be roasted as steaks or as florets. The time to cook them will be different. It takes about 15 minutes for steaks, and they need to be oiled before the oven roasting (Becky, 2021)

- Roasted vegetables make great appetizers or side plates.

Beef Brisket
Ingredients for ten servings

- Protein   Beef Brisket 4lb, first cut.

- Aromatics   Garlic 4 cloves pressed.

         Rosemary fresh four sprigs needles chopped.

         Onions red large halved.

         Tomatoes crushed one can 16 oz.

         Parsley leaves ½ cup.

         Bay Leaf 3

- Produce   Carrots cut into 3-inch chunks.

Celery stalks cut into 3-inch chunks.

- Carbohydrates   Red wine dry 2 cups

  Flour all-purpose 1 Tbsp

  Potato pancakes 20, recipe to follow.

- Fat   Olive oil ¼ cup

- Seasoning   Salt Kosher ½ teaspoon

  Black pepper, which was recently ground to taste.

For the Pancakes

- Potatoes medium 4 peeled

- two medium onions sliced lengthwise

- Kosher salt and black ground pepper to taste.

- Egg whites, two slightly beaten.

- Chives chopped finely ¼ cup.

- Canola oil for frying.

Procedure for the Beef Brisket:

1. Preheat oven to 325°F.

2. Mush and combine the garlic, salt, and rosemary leaves in a small bowl. Then add 2 Tbsp of olive oil to form a paste, stir, and liquefy if necessary. Set it aside.

3. Salt and pepper the meat liberally. Sear the beef in a Dutch oven or roasting pan with the remaining oil, allowing a nice crust to form on both sides.

4. Remove it from the heat, lay the vegetables (carrots, celery, and onions) around the brisket, and pour the rosemary paste all over the meat and vegetables.

5. Add the wine and tomatoes and toss the parsley and bay leaves. Cover the pan and transfer to the oven. Roast according to the weight using the table at the beginning of the roasting chapter and basting every 30 minutes until it reaches the internal temperature of 135°F for medium rare or 145°F for medium. I would begin checking the internal temperature often after 2 hours. If the sauce is too thin, add cornstarch slurry and boil it. You may want to strain the sauce and separate the sauce from excess fat.

6. Slice the brisket across the grain in a slant. If desired, serve with potato pancakes or taco tortillas, the sauce, and apple sauce.

Procedure for the Pancakes: two per person

1. Grate the potatoes and onions using a box grater or food processor. Mix them and squeeze out excess water using a cheesecloth or a kitchen towel. Place them in a bowl and season with salt and pepper; fold in the egg whites and chives to bind the mixture together.

2. Heat a sauteing pan with oil. For each pancake, take about a Tbsp of the potato-onion mixture, place it in the hot pan, and flatten it to cook thin and crispy (3-4 minutes on each side). They are done when golden.

3. Remove them from the pan and put them on paper towels for drainage, seasoning them with salt and pepper while

hot. Repeat the process until you run out of potato-onion chives mix.

4. Serve immediately. A sweet condiment like apple sauce or mango salsa may accompany it.

5. Alternatively, you may use taco tortillas or crepes; if you follow a low-carb diet, use chickpea flour.

Marinated Skirt Steak Inspired by Thomas Keller, (Keller, Ad Hoc at Home) (Diego, 2010) and (W&L)

Ingredients for six servings:

For the marinade:

- Aromatics   Thyme 6 sprigs

  Rosemary needles of 2 8-inch sprigs

  Bay leaves small 4.

  Black peppercorn 1 Tbsp

  Five garlic cloves pressed.

- Fat   Oil olive or canola 2 cups

Meat

- Protein   Outer skirt steaks trimmed six.

  segments 8oz each

- Seasoning   Kosher Salt and Pepper.

- Fat   Canola oil.

  Butter unsalted 2 Tbsp

- Aromatics   Thyme sprigs 4,

- Garlic cloves 2 pressed.

Skirt steaks are part of the diaphragm, the muscle that separates the chest from the belly, and have two portions. The periphery is the skirt steak, and the posterior portion that holds it to the spine is sort of like an off-center handle of an umbrella. This posterior part is the hanger steak or entraña. Both portions are lean and tough pieces of meat; without collagen, they do not benefit from prolonged cooking, are best as medium rare, and certainly not beyond medium. Always cut them across the grain (shortening the long fibers that make it tough.

Procedure:

1. Combine thyme, rosemary, bay leaves, peppercorns, garlic, and oil in a medium saucepan and bring to a simmer over medium heat. Remove from heat and let it cool to room temperature.

2. Remove the excess fat from the skirt steak and discard it. If necessary, trim the steak of any silver skin. Cut crosswise into six equal pieces.

3. Put them in a resealable plastic bag, add the marinade, remove the excess air, and seal.

4. Marinate in the refrigerator for at least 4 hours or up to a day.

5. Remove the meat from the marinade and let it sit at room temperature for 30 minutes before cooking; discard the marinade.

6. Dry the meat with paper towels—season with salt and pepper.

7. Preheat the oven to 350°F.

8. Set a roasting rack in a roasting pan.

9. Heat some canola oil in a large frying pan over high heat. (Have a splatter screen ready.) When the oil shimmers, add half the meat and quickly brown the first side. Turn the meat and, working quickly, add one tablespoon of butter, two thyme sprigs, and one garlic clove, and brown the meat on the second side, basting constantly; the entire cooking process should only take about 1 1/2 minutes. Transfer the meat to the roasting rack and spoon the butter, garlic, and thyme over the top. Wipe the pan and repeat with the remaining steaks.

10. Place the baking sheet into the oven and cook for 8 to 10 minutes (depending on how you like your steaks). Remove from the oven and let the steaks rest for about 10 minutes in a warm spot.

Bistecca a la Fiorentina Inspired by (Chiarello, 2005)

Ingredients for four servings

- Protein   2 (2-pound) Porterhouse steaks, about 2 inches thick
- Seasoning   Gray sea salt, Coarse grind black pepper
- Fat   Pure olive oil
- Condiment   Great balsamic vinegar

Procedure:

1. Leave the steak outside the refrigerator for 30 minutes before cooking. Use a hot, clean, oiled grill. If pan roasting, preheat the oven to 450 degrees F.

2. Liberally season the steak with salt and pepper, coat it with olive oil, and press the seasoning into the meat. Grill the steaks on each side for 5 to 6 minutes for medium rare. The fillet portion will cook a little faster than the strip loin part. Move the steaks every 2 minutes for even cooking and a crispy exterior.

3. Heat a cast iron skillet with some olive oil for pan roasting until smoking hot. Turn on the fan, open the window, and stand back to avoid getting splattered! Using tongs, place the steaks in the center of the pan. Cook until the first side is seared, about 4 minutes. Turn the steaks and place the pan in the oven until the steaks reach the internal temperature recommended for your liking, about 6 minutes for medium rare. Remove the steaks to a carving board and let them rest for at least 5 minutes before carving.

4. Cut the steaks from the bone and carve them into 1/2-inch slices. Arrange the meat on warmed plates and drizzle some balsamic vinegar over the slices. Serve with some extra gray sea salt on the side.

Hanger steaks with Glazed Snow Peas and Fried Cauliflower Rice Inspired by (recipe/258804/butchers-steak-hanger-steak/)

Ingredients for four servings:

- Protein   Hanger steak, four servings of 6 oz
  each

- Fat   Canola oil 2 Tbsp

- Seasoning   Kosher salt to taste

  Black pepper coarsely ground to taste, for blackening 3-4 Tbsp

For Glazed Snow Peas

- 2 tsp olive oil

- 4 cups of snow peas

- 3 Tbsp Sweet Chili Sauce

- Sea salt and freshly ground pepper to taste.

For fried cauliflower rice

Ingredients for two servings

- Fats   Vegetable oil

  Toasted sesame oil 1 tsp

- Protein   Large eggs two, beaten.

- Seasoning   Salt to taste

- Aromatics   Garlic clove 3, minced.

  Green onions, five stalks of green and white separated.

  Fresh ginger from a 1-inch knob grated.

- Condiments Soy sauce 4-5 Tbsp

  Crushed red pepper flakes ¼ teaspoon.

  Rice vinegar 1 tsp

  Sugar or stevia 1 tsp

- Produce   1 cup frozen peas and carrots
  ¼ cup chopped cashews or peanuts (optional)

  Cauliflower rice. One frozen bag, 8 oz, or a small cauliflower.

Procedure:

For the Hanger steaks:

1. Remove all silver skin and extra fat from the steak. Carefully cut out the connective tissue connecting the two halves of the steak, separating the whole into two long pieces. Rub the hanger steaks with the aromatics. Rest for about one hour.

2. Heat skillet over high heat. Add clarified butter when the pan is hot, then place the steaks. Cook only to sear on all sides. Then roast at 400°F until an instant-read thermometer inserted into the center should read 125 degrees F (52 degrees C) for about 10 minutes.) Transfer to a warm plate and tent with foil to let steaks rest and allow temperature to rise to 130 degrees F.

3. Pour the stock into the same skillet set over medium heat to prepare the pan sauce. Stir with a wooden spoon, scraping up the browned bits from the bottom. When the liquid reduces after 2 or 3 minutes, reduce the heat to low. Add the accumulated juices from the meat, balsamic vinegar, and butter chunks. Cook and stir until the butter melts. If the liquid has reduced too much, add a splash of broth. Taste to check if the sauce needs a bit

of salt. To serve, slice steaks and spoon pan sauce over them.

Roasted Hanger Steak

Hanger Steak presented as Tacos and sandwich.

For the fried cauliflower rice

Inspired by (unknown, 2024)

1. Grate the cauliflower in a food processor fitted with the grating disc. Alternatively, grate it on the large holes of

a box or hand-held grater. Set it aside. (Skip this step if using "ready-to-cook" cauliflower rice.)

2. Heat 2 teaspoons of vegetable oil in a large (10 or 12-inch) nonstick skillet over medium heat. Add the eggs and a pinch of salt and scramble until the eggs are cooked. Transfer to a small plate and set aside. Wipe the pan clean.

3. Add three tablespoons of vegetable oil to the pan and set over medium heat. Add the light scallions, garlic, and ginger and cook, stirring often, until softened but not browned, 3 to 4 minutes. Add the grated cauliflower, four tablespoons of soy sauce, red pepper flakes, sugar, and ¼ teaspoon salt. Cook, stirring often, for about 3 minutes. Add the peas and carrots and continue cooking until the cauliflower "rice" is tender-crisp and the vegetables are warmed; it should be just a few minutes. Stir in the rice vinegar, sesame oil, dark green scallions, nuts (if using) and eggs. Taste and adjust the seasoning (adding the remaining tablespoon of soy sauce if necessary). Serve hot.

For the Glazed Snow peas: do this at the last minute before serving.

1. Cut the tips off the snow peas and sauté lightly in light olive oil. Season with salt and pepper.

2. Add the sweet chili sauce to heat it until warm enough.

   Nutrition: Total fat 17g. Sat fat 11.1g total Carbs 12.3g Fiber 2.6 Protein 8.5g Calories 230

Peppered Hanger Stake with Stir-Fried Low Carb Pasta.

Ingredients for four servings:

For the meat

- Protein   4 Hanger steaks 6 oz each
- Fat   Canola oil 2 Tbsp
- Seasonings   Kosher salt to taste.

  Black pepper coarsely cracked 2 Tbsp.

For the stir-fried zero-pasta

- Carbs   Low Carb Pasta 2 10 oz bags, (Konjac pasta)
- Protein   2 large eggs beaten.
- Aromatics   Scallions 1 cup chopped and separated greens and white parts.

  Garlic 3 cloves pressed.

  Ginger grated 1 Tbsp

  Soy sauce 4 Tbsp

  Ají amarillo Powder ½ tsp

  Rice vinegar 1 tsp
- Fat   Sesame seed oil 1 tsp
- Produce   Frozen peas and carrots.
- Nuts   Cashews roasted or another nut.

Procedure:

1. Preheat the oven to 375°F. Rinse the low-carb pasta with cold water from the tap in a strainer. Divide the pasta into four servings and let them dry in the colander over a bowl.

2. You will need two hanger steaks. Divide the connective tissue that holds them together to separate them in the middle. Season the steaks liberally with salt and pepper.

3. Sear the hanger steaks in a heavy, non-stick skillet until a nice crust has formed all around, turning them as necessary.

4. Check internal temperature. The target temperature is 125-130°F. for medium rare. If it is below, place it in the oven and cook to the target temperature, usually 7-8 minutes. The most common variables are the oven settings' calibration, the steaks' thickness, and the initial temperature.

5. When ready, transfer the steaks to a cutting board and let them rest covered with foil for 10 minutes.

6. While the steaks are cooking, prepare the low-carb pasta. At medium heat, sauté the pasta; add the vegetables and aromatics when dry. In a separate pan, make an omelet and slice it into ribbons.

7. To accomplish number 6 above, add three tablespoons of vegetable oil to the pan and set over medium heat. Add the light part of the scallions, garlic, and ginger and cook, stirring often, until softened but not browned, 3 to 4 minutes. Add the pasta, four tablespoons of the soy sauce, red pepper flakes, and ¼ teaspoon salt. Cook,

stirring often, for about 3 minutes. Add the peas and carrots and continue cooking until the pasta is tender-crisp and the vegetables are warmed through, a few minutes. Stir in the rice vinegar, sesame oil, dark green scallion segments, nuts (if using), and eggs. Taste and adjust the seasoning (adding the remaining tablespoon of soy sauce if necessary). Serve hot.

Perfect Roast Beef Inspired by (Manley, how-to-make-the-perfect-roast-beef, 2023)

Because the meat used in this recipe is irregularly shaped, making it difficult to sear on the stove, we will use the technique described in the comments at the beginning of the chapter: two roasting periods at different temperatures.

Ingredients for eight servings

- Protein   Round Roast of about 4 lb.

- Fat   Canola or light olive oil 3 Tbsp

- Seasoning   Kosher salt 2 tsp

       Black Pepper coarse grounding 1 tsp

- Aromatics   Garlic pressed or grated three cloves.

       Fresh Rosemary needles 1 tbsp

       Thyme leaves 1 Tbsp

Procedure:

1. Preheat oven to 450°. Combine oil, garlic, rosemary, thyme, salt, and pepper in a small bowl. Rub all over the roast.

2. Place the roast in a roasting pan fitted with a roasting rack. Roast for 15 minutes, then reduce the heat to 325° and roast for 1 hour 45 minutes more for medium or 2 hours for medium well done. These times are for a 4lb. Roast; for different weights, see tables. *Table of Roasting times.*

3. Remove from oven and let rest 15 to 30 minutes before serving.

4. Serve with Cannellini beans and onions thickly sliced, sautéed lightly, and finished with a squirt of wine vinegar.

Smoking meats

Smoked Beef Brisket Influenced by (Laessig, 2024), and (Ford, 2022)

Ingredients:

- Whole Brisket or Packer Brisket 12- 14 lb.

- Olive oil ¼ cup

For the Rub

- 1/3 cup of Kosher salt

- 1/3 cup coarsely ground black pepper.

- 1/3 cup granulated garlic powder.

Procedure:

1. **The Day Before,** Trim excess fat from the brisket, apply olive oil, and rest. Combine the dry rub ingredients and liberally apply them to the brisket. Refrigerate overnight.

2. **On the day of cooking**, Preheat the smoker to 250°F, using the wood you prefer. When the temperature reaches 250°F, place the brisket in the smoker and insert one probe into the flat and the other into the smoker chamber.

3. When the internal temperature of the brisket is 165°F, remove it from the smoker, wrap it in Butcher paper tight, replace the probe in the general area it was before, and return it to the smoker.

4. Continue to cook at the same ambient temperature of 250°F until the meat temperature approaches 195°F (several hours 5-6). Use your instant-read thermometer to check for that buttery consistency and internal temperature in the flat and the point. A temperature of 195-205°F is done.

5. Remove from the smoker still wrapped and rest for an hour. Or place it in a cooler with no ice to hold the temperature until ready to serve.

CHAPTER 6

Method Wet High Heat

The Wet High Heat method includes Boiling, Blanching, parboiling, maceration, and shocking.

Boiling:

It is a method in which the convection of the heated water produces a bubbling effect and allows the heated air to escape for a period. While boiling occurs, the temperature of the heated liquid remains constant.

Fresh water at sea level has a boiling temperature of 212°F (100°C). The boiling temperature changes depending on the liquid used and the elevation of the locality where the boiling occurs. For example, fresh water in Denver, Colorado, boils at 202°F (94.44°C). At sea level, salted water with a salinity of seawater boils at 216.5°F (102.5°C).

The time we boil a food product varies depending on its intended use. Let's take potatoes as an example. If the intended use is potato salad, you will cook them until you can pinch them with a paring knife or fork but still feel some resistance. If you do it for purée potatoes or for mashed potatoes, you will continue boiling until you feel no resistance.

We use boiling for soups or preparing a food product that will be finished with other cooking methods.

Purée Potatoes Recipe Inspired by (Sylvie, 2019) and (Keller, Master Classes Thomas Keller Technics 1 Vegetables) (Stewat)

Ingredients for four servings

- 6 1/2/ oz (190 grams) of cream. Hot.

- 1 cup (225 grams) cold butter.

- 3 ½ Tbsp (cubed 50 grams) clarified butter (optional)

- 1lb. 10 oz (750 grams) Yukon Gold potatoes

- Warm water as needed.

- Kosher salt

- Butter for finishing

- Maldon salt for finishing

Procedure:

1. Place the unpeeled potatoes in a 3-quart saucepot and cover by 2 inches with cold water. Slowly bring the water to a gentle simmer. Cook the potatoes whole to prevent them from absorbing the water and, therefore, allow you to incorporate more butter and cream. Cook the potatoes until they are incredibly tender when assessed with a paring knife and encounter no resistance.

2. Working one potato at a time, remove it from the water, place it on the tamis, split it in half, and press the flesh

through the screen using a stiff bowl scraper, leaving the skins behind.

3. Transfer them to a 4-quart saucepan. Warm the saucepan over medium-low heat; use a stiff rubber spatula to incorporate 1/3 of the hot cream into the potatoes. Beat in a few butter cubes with the rubber spatula until the butter is emulsified into the potatoes. Drizzle in a little clarified butter if used. Clarified butter adds a more intense butter flavor than whole butter.

4. Add the cream, butter, and clarified butter to develop a creamy purée. The ideal pommes purée should have a milky, creamy appearance. If the purée looks oily, with the fat separating from the potatoes, the emulsion has begun to break. To restore the emulsion, you may need to add hot water periodically, just as you would for mayonnaise or hollandaise.

5. Regulate the heat to incorporate the butter without losing the emulsion; once you have achieved your desired texture, season with salt, transfer to a serving bowl, and top with a pad of butter.

Are purée potatoes different than mashed potatoes? Yes, in mashed potatoes, you use a ricer instead of a tamis; the amount of butter and cream used is significantly less, and the consistency is not as smooth. Both are delicious; it is an individual preference to see which one you like better.

Minestrone with a Peruvian Touch

Minestrone is a vegetable soup in most places, but in Perú, it is prepared with pieces of short ribs included.

Ingredients for four servings

- Protein   Short ribs, boneless and cut in large cubes.

  Parmesan cheese is grated, not pre-grated.

- Carbohydrates   Rigatoni or Penne pasta. 2 cups.

- Aromatics   Onion 1 cup cubed medium.

  Leeks cubed 1 cup

  Garlic 6 cloves pressed.

  Carrots 1 cup cubed.

  Tomato paste 2 tbsp

- Produce   Green beans, cut in a slant 1 cup.

  Baby Lima Beans dried 1 cup soaked overnight.

Potatoes peeled and cubed into large cubes 1 cup.

Yucca peeled and cubed into large cubes 1 cup.

Cabbage chopped 1 cup.

Corn kernels 1 cup.

Zucchini seeded and cubed medium 1 cup.

- Liquid   Beans soaking liquid 4 cups.

  Water or vegetable broth 4 cups.

- Flavorings Pesto

- Seasoning Salt and pepper to taste after beans cooked.

For the Pesto

- Fat   Extra virgin olive oil

- Aromatics Onion red cubed medium.

  Garlic 2 cloves pressed.

  Basil Leaves 1 cup.

  Spinach leaves 1 cup of Italian parsley.

- Season   Kosher salt and pepper to taste.

For the Soffrito

- Red Onion ½ cubed small.
- Carrots 2 medium, cubed small.
- Leeks cubed small, ½ cup.
- Celery 1 stalk cubed small.
- Light olive oil or canola oil, 3 Tbsp

Procedure:

1. The night before, soak the lima beans in 4 cups of water, or enough to cover them.

2. Prepare il soffrito. Heat a medium to small saucepan with a liberal amount of light olive oil,

   When shimmering, add the remaining ingredients at medium-low heat and cook them slowly until caramelized about 45 minutes.

3. Meanwhile, in a large pot, heat the 4 cups of bean-soaking water and parboil the short ribs until ½ halfway cooked. Then add the soffrito and the aromatics, lima beans, potatoes, and yucca. Cook them until they are soft but not fully cooked.

4. Add the remaining vegetables (cabbage, corn kernels, zucchini, and green beans). Cook until the green beans are done. Check the lima beans; they should be soft, creamy, and ready to burst.

5. Add the pesto, and the Parmesan cheese. Serve while hot.

Blanching

It is the process of **improving the color of vegetables** by releasing a layer of gas between the pigment and the skin. (Keller, Master Classes Thomas Keller Technics 1 Vegetables)

If you wait too long and the vegetables get overcooked, their color will dull because acid and enzymes bleach out. The vegetable's texture is a matter of preference; the most pleasing is to have a bit of a crunch left on it.

The timing of how long to blanch a vegetable depends significantly on the vegetable itself, and I will mention that in the following recipes.

The liquid to blanch a vegetable should be in a large stockpot, so adding the vegetables will not stop the boiling. The water for boiling should be heavily salted, about the same as seawater. Sea water has about 3.3 grams of salt per 100 ml, or about 3 Tbsp per liter (1 Tbsp = 13.8 g).

Blanch vegetables when they become snacks in vegetable trays with dips, crudités, and salads or when they are to be finished with a different cooking method.

Blanching Asparagus

Ingredients for four servings

- Asparagus 5-6 per serving, depending on size and thickness, cleaned and trimmed.

- Stockpot with an abundant amount of water.

- Salt about sea water concentration 3.3 g. per 100 cc

Procedure:

1. Boil a large pot of water. Once boiling, add the appropriate amount of salt, dissolve the salt, and heat further until the water boils with the added salt.

2. Bundle the asparagus in groups of 2 servings; add just enough asparagus to maintain a rapid boil. Check with a paring knife for tenderness at 2 ½ minutes; boil more if necessary.

3. You may need multiple batches. As soon as you remove them from the pot, ***shock them in ice water* to stop them from continuing to cook**.

4. You may serve them directly or as part of a complete dinner dish.

5. Blanching may be a step in preparing the asparagus to be finished, for example, with a different cooking method like grilling or broiling.

Blanching Green Beans

Ingredients:

- Green beans prep by snapping the ends, avoiding exposing the contents.

- Blanching in a large pot of salted water. A similar concentration of salt as seawater.

- Ice bath for shocking after boiling the green beans, and prep while water begins to boil.

Procedure:

1. Place the pot with salted water to boil.

2. While simmering, prepare your ice bath for shocking.

3. When the water is at a hard boiling, add a portion of the green beans so the boiling does not stop.

4. Boil the green beans for 3 minutes; remove and shock them.

5. Work with another batch of green beans until finished.

6. Remove the green beans from the ice water when cool and place them in a bowl.

7. When completed, keep them in a cool place wrapped in paper towels to dry. Then, to complete the dish, serve them with a sauce of your choice.

8. This step may be followed by finishing them with a different cooking method, like sauteing with garlic.

Blanching Other vegetables

The differences will be in the vegetable prep and the blanching time.

Prep the **Broccoli** by splitting the main stem and cutting the flower into evenly sized florets. Blanch them for 1 minute. Notice the color difference.

Cauliflower: Cut it into quarters along the main stem. Slice the thick main stem away, and the florets will fall from the stem. Blanch the florets for three to five minutes.

Baby Carrots, split them in quarters lengthwise and cook them for 1 minute.

Shock all of them in ice water until they are completely chilled, about 3 minutes. Then, arrange them on a platter to serve with a dip, cover them lightly, and refrigerate them later.

Parboiling

Parboiling or leaching consists of partially or semi-boiling food products as the first step in cooking. Unlike blanching, which involves shocking the food in ice water, parboiling does not involve shocking the food after removal from the boiling liquid. Therefore, the food is cooked more than in blanching. Another difference is that while the water is boiling in blanching, parboiling is more of a simmer than hard boiling.

The technique is similar: you add the food to the boiling water and cook it until it softens, then remove it before it is fully cooked. The cooking of the food product is completed by a different method, like roasting, braising, grilling, stir or deep frying. Parboiling shortens the time of the next cooking process, particularly if cooking several products with different cooking times allows them to be finished simultaneously. For example, in soups with meats and vegetables, start with the meats and add the vegetables later so neither will be overcooked.

Another effect is that it changes the quality of the food product. For example, parboiling potatoes to roast them later makes the roasted potatoes crispier and more golden in color. The same applies to French-fried potatoes or roasted chicken.

Parboiled Roasted Potatoes

Based on J Kinji López-Alt recommendations *(Lopez, 2022)*

The roasting process begins with choosing the potatoes (russet or gold Yukon), peeling them, and cutting them into large chunks (to increase the ratio of crispy outside and creamy center). Then, parboil them, followed by simmering until there is little resistance when tested with the tip of a paring knife. Then, dry them (resting in the empty hot pan) and flavor them with oil, aromatics, and flavorings.

- Carbohydrates   Potatoes (russet or Yukon gold) peeled and cut.

- Seasonings   Kosher salt and 2 Tbsp

                                Ground pepper to taste.

                                Baking soda ½ tsp

- Flavorings   Fresh Rosemary leaves,

                                finely chopped.

                                Garlic minced ½ Tbsp

                                Fresh parsley leaves are finely
                                chopped.

- Fat   Olive oil light 6 Tbsp

Procedure:

1. Preheat oven to 450°F or 400°F with convection.

2. Heat a large pot with 2 quarts of water or more; add the Kosher salt (2 Tbsp), Baking soda (½ tsp), and potato chunks once boiling. Return to a boil, then reduce heat to a simmer until testing with the tip of the paring knife offers little resistance (about 10-12 minutes after returning to a boil.

3. Heat the oil in a small saucepan and add the garlic (minced) and rosemary until the garlic turns golden. Separate the oil from the solids through a fine sieve and set both aside separately (maceration, flavoring the liquid).

4. When the potatoes are done, drain the salty water and keep them in the hot pot for a minute to allow them to dry.

5. Transfer the potatoes to the Infused oil, cover them with plastic wrap, and shake them hard until a layer of potato-paste settles on the chunks' surfaces.

6. Spread the potatoes on a baking sheet in a single layer and roast them for 20 minutes undisturbed; at the 20-minute mark, turn them over and continue to roast until they turn deep brown in color and crisp. Shake them during this time several times (30-40 additional minutes).

7. Transfer to a bowl, add the rosemary garlic mixture kept aside, and the minced parsley.

8. Serve while hot.

French fries Recipe
Inspired by (Lopez-Alt K.)

Ingredients:

• Carbohydrates	Potatoes peeled and cut into ¼-by-¼ inch 2 lbs.
• Vinegar white distilled	2 Tbsp
• Kosher Salt	2 tbsp for parboiling and additional for sprinkling.
• Peanut oil	2 quarts.

Procedure:

1. Parboil potatoes: Add the potatoes, water, vinegar, and salt and bring to a boil. Boil for 10 minutes. The potatoes should be tender but not breaking up. Drain them and allow them to dry on paper towels.

2. heat oil in a 5-quart Dutch oven or electric deep fryer to 400°F; cook parboiled potatoes for 50 seconds, and

remove to a paper towel-lined rimmed baking sheet. Allow the temperature to return to 400°F before doing the next batch. Let them cool and freeze overnight or for up to 2 months.

3. When ready to finish, return the oil to 400°F. Fry the potatoes in batches for about 3 ½ minutes, adjusting the temperature to maintain 360°F while cooking them and returning to 400°F between batches. Season immediately with salt and serve.

Cooking Rice

Cooking rice in the Peruvian style involves sequential sauteing, parboiling, and steaming. We call this method Pilaf style. We are presenting it now because several recipes often use it as a side dish.

Rice is cooked when the temperature reaches a point where the crystalline structures of the starch begin to melt. This is called gelatinization temperature (GT), and it ranges between 131°F-55°C and 185°F-85°C.

Methods: Most methods depend on the proportion of water and rice. Generally, the longer the rice grain, the fluffier the final product; the shorter the grain, the stickier the final product. Some methods use excess water, discarding it after the rice is cooked; others use an optimal amount of water, which varies according to the type of rice used. The rice can be boiled, steamed, or cooked using a combination.

I prefer to use an optimum amount of water (1 cup rice to 1½ cups water of long grain), pilaf style, a combination of sautéed, boiled, and steamed. The definition of pilaf style is problematic because it is prepared in diverse ways around the world. We use the term as a basic rice pilaf made by sautéing, usually long grain rice in butter, oil, or both, and some pressed garlic and salt. Sauté until the rice browns slightly, and then add whatever broth you want or water. It also works for shorter-grain rice, basmati, or jasmine rice.

Example recipe *Rice Pilaf method of Cooking Rice*

INSTRUCTIONS

In a tea kettle, heat the water to boiling.

1. In an adequate-size saucepan, place 1 Tbsp of oil, a tsp of pressed garlic, and 1 tsp of salt for each cup of rice. Oil should be of high smoking temperature, like canola or avocado oils (to prevent the formation of trans-fats from excessive heat). Add the amount of rice chosen and toast it for a few minutes.

2. Then add the proportional amount of hot water or broth needed; the ratio is 1.5 to 1 of water to rice by volume.

3. With the saucepan uncovered, boil the mixture until you can see little volcanoes erupting from the rice surface or

Ready to reduce heat and cover.   *Fully cooked, ready to be fluffed with a fork.*

like molten lava. (**Parboiling**) At this point, turn the heat to extremely low, cover the saucepan with a lid, leave a little vent, and **steam** for 18 minutes. Fluff the rice with a fork, turn the heat off, and serve.

Example Recipe

Chicken and Rice, Peruvian Style

Uses cilantro and ají amarillo as flavorings, as opposed to saffron in the classical Spanish Arroz con Pollo. Another difference is the type of rice used.

Ingredients for four servings

- **Herbs and spices** : 1 cup cilantro leaves or

  1 Tbsp cilantro paste or Pesto (*Pesto)*

  1 tsp ground cumin

  One bay leaf

- **Season with** Kosher Salt and pepper to taste.

- **Aromatics:** 1 small onion, diced small

  cloves of garlic, minced 3.

  2 tsp ají Amarillo

- **Simmering liquid:** 1 ½ cup beer or white wine

  1 ½ cup chicken broth

- **Vegetables:** 2 small carrots, diced small

  small red pepper diced small one.

  peas 2 cups.

  corn kernels 1 cup

	scallions chopped 5
Rice, long grain	2 cup (basmati, jasmine is okay)
Chicken	4 chicken legs and thighs

Procedure:

1. Pulse cilantro leaves and 2 Tbsp of water till smooth in a food processor.

2. Sauté to brown the chicken in a pan with some oil. Set it aside.

3. Cook the onions, garlic, cumin, and ají amarillo low and slow until the onion is translucent; do not brown.

4. Add the simmering liquids and scrape to free the fond residue from browning the chicken in the bottom of the pan or skillet.

5. Add the bay leaf.

6. Add the sautéed chicken, vegetables, pureed cilantro, salt, and pepper. Cover and simmer for 15 minutes.

7. Add the rice, cover, and simmer for 20 minutes until the rice is done.

8. Add the peas and corn kernels if frozen for a couple of minutes before finished; otherwise, add them with the rice.

Parboiling Meats

Parboiling is cooking a food product partially, different from blanching, which aims to improve the color of the vegetable by releasing the gases between the color pigment and the membrane of the vegetable cell and maintaining the vegetable's crunch. You must stop cooking and shock the vegetable in ice water to achieve blanching. In parboiling, the objective is to cook the food product partially, aiming for a shorter cooking time when finishing later and improving the quality of the finished dish.

Meats often parboiled include chicken, ribs, brats, and sausages. We complete their cooking later by grilling, roasting, simmering, or frying with a final product that is crispy on the surface, juicy, and fully cooked in the center.

The parboiling times vary with the type of meat and the size of the pieces. A whole chicken (30-40 minutes) will take longer than a breast (10 minutes), a thigh (5 minutes), or a sausage (8 minutes).

Maceration

It is the process where solids (meats, vegetables, fats) are cooked to flavor the cooking liquid. Ultimately, you may or may not discard the solids and serve the liquid. The cook uses this method to prepare broths and soups. Infusions are like beverages (steeping) like tea, coffee, and chocolate.

The recipe of *Minestrone with a Peruvian touch* in the Boiling Method (*Minestrone with a Peruvian Touch*) is an excellent example of maceration, in which the meat and vegetables infuse their flavors into the liquid while cooking and are kept in the final dish.

CHAPTER 7

Wet Low Heat Methods

Coddling

Coddling an egg is like poaching an egg, but instead of cooking the egg in the water/vinegar mix, you place the egg in a recipient (ramekin) seasoned and then put in the hot water to cook. Alternate methods include placing the ramekin in the microwave for 1- 1 ½ minutes at the lowest power possible—in my microwave, it's 1 minute at 40% power—to cook the white and yolk and make them a bit runny. Alternatively, you can place the egg in a plastic bag, eliminating all the air by submerging it in water just before zip-locking it and then using the sous vide equipment.

Raw seasoned eggs in ramekins.   After microwave cooking

Poaching (Ang, 2018)

Poaching is a wet, low-heat cooking method by heating food submerged in a liquid at a temperature below boiling, usually between 158°F (70°C) and 176 °F (80°C); the temperature will vary depending on the liquid used.

Poaching differs from other wet methods like boiling or simmering, where the temperatures are higher, at near or boiling temperatures. This makes poaching suitable for delicate food products such as eggs, fish, poultry, and fruits.

Poaching will denature the proteins without pooling too much water out of the food or too much flavor. This makes it essential to keep temperatures low and time short to prevent excessive maceration. The liquid, when reduced, is used to make sauces for the dish being prepared.

Poaching can be Shallow Poaching, where the liquid does not cover the food product, and the pan is covered to combine poaching and steaming. This way, we minimize the loss of flavor to the liquid, and the preparation from the liquid requires less reduction. Deep Poaching is where the liquid entirely covers the food product; the degree of doneness is determined by the internal temperature of 150-165°F. for chicken and 115-120°F for fish. The deep poaching method can begin with a cold liquid and be brought to a temperature of 170°F, maintaining that temperature until the internal temperature reaches the level of the desired doneness. Or it starts with the liquid already heated to a poaching temperature, and there are supporters for both techniques.

Poached Eggs

Poaching eggs has been around for a long time, and multiple different techniques are described, such as swirling the poaching liquid to help the egg white wrap around the yolk. Often, there are stringy attachments around the periphery that need trimming. This happens because there are two components to the egg white: about 90% water, into which about 10% proteins (including albumins, mucoproteins, and globulins) are in solution. The distribution is not even; the periphery is more aqueous, and the central part is richer in proteins, primarily albumin. The stringy formations that sometimes appear while poaching are formed from the more diluted portion of the egg white. On Instagram, a video by Natasha Kravchuk (Kravchuk, 2024) It made a lot of sense. I will describe this method.

Ingredients:

- Eggs   2 eggs, do not need to be room temp.

- Water   enough to cover the eggs.

- Distilled vinegar   1 Tbsp

Procedure:

1. Place the water and vinegar in a saucepan. Bring the temperature to around 170°F, but do not boil it. If heating it covered, as it starts to break into a boil, uncover the pot and lower the heat. The temperature will be exactly right.

2. Strain each egg separately in a medium-mesh strainer. The more aqueous portion of the egg whites will go

through the strainer; the thicker portion will remain in the strainer with the yolk. Transfer the egg to a ladle; if it is a metal ladle, spray it with cooking spray and place it in the poaching solution, allowing a bit of poaching liquid into the ladle. As soon as you see a little film of egg white solidifying, slip the egg into the saucepan. 4-5 minutes, depending on your taste and the temperature of the poaching liquid. It will produce a perfect poached egg.

Poached egg.

Poached egg, runny yolk.

Poached Salmon with Dill Yogurt Sauce inspired by (Gritzer, poached-salmon-dill-yogurt-sauce-recipe, 2016)

Ingredients for four servings:

For the poached Salmon

- Protein   Salmon filets center cut, four 8oz filets.

- Liquid   Water, enough to cover the

salmon filets.

- Flavorings Lemon Juice 2 Tbsp

  Onion or leek medium, halved.

  The celery stalk was cut into large segments one stalk.

  Fennel sliced ½ a bulb.

  Thyme and/or Dill 3-4 sprigs.

  Bay leaf one.

- Seasoning Kosher salt in one large pinch.

For the Yogurt Sauce

- Full-fat yogurt 1 cup.

- Shallot minced 1 Tbsp

- Fresh dill minced 1 Tbsp

- Lemon Juice 2 Tbsp

- Extra Virgin olive oil 2 Tbsp

- Coriander seeds ground in one large pinch.

- Kosher salt and ground black pepper to taste.

- Ají Amarillo 2 tsp

Procedure:

1. In a large saucepan, combine the water (start with one quart), the seasoning (salt, one large pinch), and the flavorings (lemon juice, leek or onion, celery, fennel,

thyme, dill, and bay leaf). Add the salmon filets. If the solution does not cover the fish, add enough water to do so.

2. Heat the poaching solution on medium heat and adjust to keep it close to 170°F but not above. Cook until the internal temperature reaches 115°F.

3. Transfer the salmon to a plate and rest for about 5 minutes.

For the Yogurt Dill sauce

1. Mix all the ingredients in a small bowl. Stir until homogeneous.

May serve the salmon while warm, at room temperature, or refrigerated and cold.

Poaching a la Nage

Poaching a la Nage is a form of shallow poaching (the food product is only partially covered by the poaching liquid). You cover the pan so it combines poaching with steaming (the top part of the fish or shellfish is not submerged, so it will cook by steaming). The liquid is a light broth acidified by white wine or lemon juice. (PoachingalaNage).

How to Cook *À La Nage*

1. Sauté vegetables, such as garlic, onions, fennel, and celery, in oil or butter until the mixture turns transparent.

2. Add a poaching mixture of white wine, water, and fish stock to the pot.

3. Gently lower the fish into the broth, making sure it partially submerges the fish.

4. Bring the broth to a simmer, cover the pot, and continue cooking slowly.

5. When the fish is fully cooked, at an Internal temperature of 115°F, the dish is ready.

Daniel Gritzer of www.seriouseats.com suggests several variations of fish prepared á la Nage, where changes in a few ingredients produce a different dish. His recommendations have inspired some of the recipes that follow.

Sudado de Corvina or Shallow Poached Corvina á la Nage Inspired by (Gritzer, salmon-a-la-nage, 2022)

This is a classic Peruvian dish that uses the technique of Shallow poaching á la Nage, which combines poaching and steaming the fish. The fish is cooked in a fish broth augmented by aromatics and herbs.

Ingredients for four servings:

- Protein   4 filets of corvina center cut 6 oz

                              each.

- Carbohydrates   Yukon potato large, boiled, cut into

                              thick slices

                              Rice Peruvian style 2 cups cooked.

- Fat   Canola oil 2 Tbsp

- Seasonings   Sea Salt to taste.

  Black Pepper to taste.

- Aromatics   Red onion one cubed large

  Garlic 3 cloves pressed.

  Ají amarillo paste 2 Tbsp

  Tomatoes concasse three grated

  Tomato paste 1 Tbsp

  Cilantro sprigs 4

  Poaching liquid

  The fish stock is 3 cups, just enough to cover the fish partially.

  White wine ¼ cup.

Procedure:

1. Heat the oil at medium heat, add the aromatics, and prepare a sofrito low and slow.

2. Incorporate the fish stock, white wine, and cilantro sprigs, bring to a boil, turn the heat low, and cover tightly. Cook for 10-15 minutes to incorporate all the flavors.

3. Season the fillets with salt and pepper, add them to the saucepan, and poach them at 170°F or slightly lower until the fish reaches an internal temperature of 115-120°F, about 5-7 minutes, depending on thickness.

4. Serve fish with sauce over rice and potato slices.

Mero a la Chorrillana or Poached Grouper á la Nage

This is another Peruvian dish from the Pacific coast just south of Lima. It uses the shallow poaching technique, which combines poaching and steaming with the added step of sauteing the fish to a golden crust.

Ingredients for two servings:

- Protein   Grouper filet proximal and center cut two- 6 oz each.

- Fat   1/3 cup canola oil, divided.

  Mayonnaise 2 tsp

- Carbohydrates   Rice cooked 1 ½ cups.

- Aromatics   Onion red 2 cut into thick slices.

  Garlic 3 cloves, pressed.

  Ají amarillo paste 1 tbsp

  Tomato concasse one tomato chopped.

  Tomatoes 2 sliced thick.

  Cilantro leaves chopped, 2 tbsp

  Oregano dried, 1 tsp

- Seasonings   Sea Salt and Black ground pepper to taste.

- Poaching liquid   Red wine vinegar ¼ cup

    Fish or vegetable stock ½ cup.

Procedure:

In this dish, we do not want to prepare the classic sofrito like a mirepoix, where the aromatics are cooked low and slow, stopping before browning or caramelizing. Here, we don't want the onions to lose their crunch, so we cook them at high temperatures and avoid browning or caramelizing by adding the liquids, vinegar, and broth.

1. Prepare the fish by brushing its surfaces with mayonnaise, salting lightly, and sprinkling with freshly ground black pepper. Sauté the fish in 2 Tbsp of oil to brown the surfaces. Remove it from the pan and set aside.

2. Prepare the sauce: Place the remainder of the canola oil in a saucepan, add the aromatics except the tomato slices and cilantro, turn the heat up to maximum, cook for about a minute, add tomato slices, turn the heat down to low, add the poaching liquid just enough to cover the fish partially, then add the reserved fish, cover tightly, and cook at a low simmer until the fish's internal temperature reaches 115°F.

3. Place a piece of fish on each plate, cover with sauce and vegetables, accompanied with rice, and garnish with cilantro.

MERO A LA CHORRILLANA

Thai Flavored Cod á La Nage

Ingredients for four servings

- Protein   Cod Filets, skinless, Four -6 oz each
- Aromatics   Shallots minced small.

  Garlic 3 cloves pressed.

  Ají Amarillo paste 2 tsp

- Flavoring   Ginger grated 2 inches.

  Lime peel 3 – 2inches

  Lemon grass cut into 3-inch segments, bruised.

  Cilantro 2 sprigs.

  Basil 2 sprigs

- Seasoning   Kosher salt and freshly ground black

- Poaching Liquid   Coconut Milk –Two 14 oz cans.

                                   Fish sauce Thai 2 tsp

- Finishing sauce   Lime juice 2 Tbsp

Procedure:

1. Sauté aromatics until shallots are translucent (shallots, garlic, and ají amarillo paste).

2. Add the poaching liquids and the flavorings (coconut milk and fish sauce).

3. Season the fish with salt and pepper, then gently lower it into the pot. It should be only partially submerged. Bring the liquid to a simmer, cover, reduce the heat, and cook until the internal temperature of the fish reaches 115°F. Remove from the heat.

4. Place the fish in bowls, add the lime juice to the poaching liquid, stir, and serve the sauce around the fish with the vegetables. By then, the internal temperature of the fish should be the safe temperature for fish meat 125-130°F.

Poached Grouper á la Nage with Vegetables Bowl

(RecipesDanielGritzer)

Ingredients for four servings

- Protein   Grouper filets proximal and center cuts

                                   Four – 6oz each.

- Fats

    Light olive oil 2 Tbsp

    Extra virgin olive oil 1 Tbsp

- Aromatics

    Carrots, medium, diced 2.

    Fennel bulb, small, diced 1.

    Summer squash, small 2.

    Zucchini diced small 2.

    Onion red, medium, cubed medium ½.

    Ginger peeled, grated 2-inch segment.

- Flavorings

    Parsley 2 sprigs, Tarragon 2 sprigs

    Ají amarillo, paste 2 tsp

- Poaching liquid

    White wine dry, 1 cup.

    Water or fish stock 3 cups

- Seasonings

    Kosher salt and freshly ground black pepper to taste.

- For salad

    Cherry tomatoes, split lengthwise 1 cup.

    Green onions, white and light green parts only, cut in a slant, two stalks.

- Garnishing

    Parsley and Tarragon, chopped 2 Tbsp

Procedure:

1. Sauté the Aromatics in light olive oil until the onions become transparent.

2. Add the wine and cook off the alcohol. Then add the water or fish broth. Add the flavorings.

3. Season the grouper filets with salt and pepper. Slide the filets into the poaching liquid; they should be partially submerged, about 2/3 of the thickness. Bring the poaching liquid to a simmer, cover, and lower the heat to keep a slow simmer or just below. Cook until the internal temperature at the thickest portion of the fillets reaches 115-120°F, about 4-5 minutes.

4. Meanwhile, toss tomatoes, green onions, and one tablespoon of extra virgin olive oil in a bowl—season with salt and pepper.

5. Serve with the groper at the center of the bowl, surrounded by the vegetables from the poaching pot. Distribute the salad around and garnish with chopped parsley and tarragon.

Poached Halibut á la Nage with Clams (RecipesDanielGritzer)

Ingredients for four servings:

- Protein   Halibut fillets, skinless, 4– 6oz each.

  Little neck clams, one dozen.

- Fats   Butter unsalted 4 Tbsp divided by 2.

- Aromatics   Yellow onion, medium, diced

  medium size.

  Fennel, small, diced.

  Garlic 3 cloves pressed.

  Celery 1 stalk, diced.

Ají amarillo paste 2 tsp

- Seasoning   Sea salt and freshly ground black Pepper to taste.

- Poaching Liquid   White wine dry, 1 cup. Water 2 cups.

- For sauce   Remaining butter Dill leaves, chopped 1 Tbsp

Procedure:

1. Melt 2 Tbsp of butter in a saucepan. When foaming, add the aromatics. Cook at medium heat until onions are translucent, stirring intermittently.

2. Add wine and allow it to burn; the alcohol should be reduced by half. Add water and bring to a simmer. Meanwhile, season the fish fillets with salt and pepper, then slide them in the poaching liquid and nestle the clams around the fish. Cover tightly and lower the heat to keep a gentle simmer.

3. When the clams are open and the fish's internal temperature registers 115-120°F, turn the heat off. Set the plates for serving. Transfer the fish and clams to bowls, then add the dill and remaining butter to the poaching liquid, whisking until the butter is melted.

4. Then, ladle the sauce and vegetables into the bowls and serve.

Poached Halibut in Coconut Broth (Alex, 2021)
Ingredients for two servings:

- Protein   Halibut fillet, skinless, cut into Two pieces.

- Fat   Avocado oil 2 Tbsp

- Aromatics large   Shallot large one diced in cubes.

  Garlic 3 cloves, pressed.

  Ginger 1 inch peeled and grated.

- For Poaching liquid   Coconut Milk 13 oz can, one.

  Seafood stock 1 cup.

  Fish sauce 1 Tbsp

  Coconut aminos 1 Tbsp

  Zest of 1 lime

  Lime juice 2 Tbsp

  Sugar 1 Tbsp

  Ají amarillo paste 2 tsp

  Coriander seeds ground ¼ tsp

Produce: Shitake mushrooms 4oz sliced.

                                         Snow peas 2 cups

- Carbohydrates   White rice cooked.

Procedure:

1. Sauté the aromatics in the avocado oil, season with salt, and cook until the shallot is translucent.

2. Add the poaching liquid ingredients. Bring to a simmer.

3. Add the produce and the fish; they should be covered entirely. Cook at a slow simmer until the fish is done, flakes easily, and the internal temperature is 120-125°F, about 5-6 minutes.

4. Serve over white or brown rice and some poaching liquid. Garnish with scallions and cilantro leaves.

Poached Salmon Bowl
(MarthaStewartpotatosalad)

Ingredients for four servings

- Protein   Salmon Filet with skin 1 lb.

- Fat   Ghee 6 Tbsp

- Carbohydrates   Fingerling potatoes split lengthwise. 1 lb.

- Seasoning   Kosher salt 1 Tbsp + to taste.

  Black pepper freshly ground to taste.

  Maldon sea salt for finishing.

- Aromatics   Shallot minced small, 2 Tbsp

Mint leaves ½ cup,

Baby Spinach leaves trimmed, washed, and spun dry, 8oz

Dijon Mustard 1 tsp

Ají amarillo 1 tsp if desired.

- Poaching liquid   Sherry vinegar 3 Tbsp

  Water is enough to cover the potatoes and then the salmon.

Procedure:

1. In a saucepan, boil the potatoes in cold tap water, enough to cover them. Add a Tbsp of salt, and when they can be pierced with a paring knife with ease but with some residual resistance, remove them from the water with a slotted spoon to a bowl and cover to keep warm.

2. Season the salmon filet with salt and pepper. Place the poaching liquid in a skillet and bring it to poaching temperature. Then, slide the salmon filet into the poaching liquid and add water to cover it. Bring it back to a slow boil, remove it from the heat, cover it, and rest until the internal temperature at the thickest part of the fillet reaches 115°F. Transfer to a plate, skin side up, and cover with a foil tent.

3. Prepare the sauce/dressing by melting the ghee in a saucepan. Remove it from the heat when it turns golden brown, and immediately whisk in the shallot, mustard,

Ají amarillo, and vinegar (pre-mixed). It will spatter. Cover to keep warm.

4. Toss the potatoes with the spinach, mint, and ½ - 2/3 of the vinaigrette. Remove the skin of the filet, drizzle the remainder of the vinaigrette on the fish, flake the fish in large pieces, and divide it with the potato spinach salad in 4 serving bowls.

Poached Cod in Lemongrass Broth over Baby Spinach Inspired by (Fountain, 2017)

Ingredients for two servings

- Protein   Cod 8 oz filet. Cut in 2

- Fat   Coconut oil 2 tsp

- Aromatics   Shallot, large one diced small.

  Garlic cloves, 3 pressed.

  Lemon grass paste ¼ cup, divided.

  Ginger, grated, 1-inch knob.

  Ají amarillo paste 1 tsp

- Poaching Liquid   Fish sauce, 2 tsp

  Chicken or fish stock 4 cups

  ½ cup coconut milk.

  Juice of 1 lime

  2 tsp of Ají amarillo paste.

- Vegetables   5 oz Baby spinach.

Shitake Mushrooms 8.Kefir Lime leaves sliced.

Procedure:

1. Prep the Fish by seasoning with salt and pepper.

2. Sauté, in the coconut oil, the aromatics but only half of the divided lemongrass paste.

3. Add the stock, fish sauce, and a 3-finger pinch of salt. Simmer for 5 minutes for flavors to meld, then add the coconut milk, ají amarillo, and lime juice. This can be made ahead and refrigerated.

4. Slide the fish in the simmering poaching liquid for 2-3 minutes, spoon the liquid over the fish, and check the internal temperature of the fish, at 115-120°F, then it is done.

5. Serve by placing half of the spinach in each bowl. Place the fish over the spinach with a slotted spatula and ladle the poaching liquid over the fish and spinach. Garnish with thin slices of radishes. Serve it hot.

Butter Poached Fish.
Inspired by (Manley, Butter Poached Fish, 2020)

Ingredients for two servings:

- Protein   White flesh fish

- Fat   Unsalted butter or ghee 6 oz

- Liquid   1-2 Tbsp lemon juice

- Aromatics   Shallots minced small dice 1 Tbsp

Ají amarillo paste 1 tsp

Fresh herbs Cilantro, chives, thyme.

Procedure:

1. Sauté the aromatics in two Tbsp of butter or ghee until shallots are translucent.

2. Add lemon juice and the remaining butter or ghee. When the butter or ghee has melted, slide in the fish. It should be 2/3 of the thickness submerged. If not, add more lemon juice, butter, or water. Cook for 3 minutes. If the poaching liquid begins to boil, turn the heat down and cook for another minute. Check the internal temperature of the fish. If it registers 115-120°F, then it is done.

3. Serve while hot with a Tbsp of the poaching liquid and shallots.

Poached Chicken Breasts

Ingredients for two servings:

- Protein   boneless, skinless Chicken Breasts 2

- Poaching liquid   Chicken broth low sodium 1 ½ - 2 cups.

  Dried mixed herbs (Italian, Provence, etc.).

  Bay leaf 1.

- Aromatics   Red Onion, small, cubed medium.

Garlic 2 cloves, pressed.

Ají amarillo paste 1 tsp

- Fat   Ghee 1 Tbsp

Procedure:

1. Sauté the aromatics in the ghee until the onion is translucent.

2. Add the chicken breasts and sauté to golden.

3. Add the poaching liquid; the chicken should be covered. Bring to a boil and quickly reduce to a slow simmer, a temperature of about 170°F for the poaching liquid. Poach for about 15-20 minutes to an internal temperature of 160-165°F.

These chicken breasts can be used for soups, chicken salads, sandwiches, or tacos. The poaching liquid can be used for soups or to cook dry beans.

You may cook chicken thighs the same way, but they will require longer poaching times to reach an internal temperature of 160°F.

To serve with homemade Hollandaise sauce:

Ingredients:

- two large egg yolks

- 1 Tbsp of lemon juice

- ½ Tbsp of water

- 8 Tbsp ghee melted.

- one two-finger pinch of salt or to taste.

Procedure:

1. In the bottom of a double boiler, bring about one inch of water to a simmer (not boil).

2. Whisk the egg yolks with the lemon juice and ½ Tbsp of water at the top of the double boiler.

3. Place the top over the simmering water. Whisk continuously until the mixture is warm and begins to thicken.

4. Slowly whisk the melted ghee into the egg yolk mixture. Cook over simmering water, whisking continuously, until the sauce has thickened. Remove from the heat, and add salt and ají amarillo powder, if desired.

5. Keep warm, covered in an oven preheated at the lowest temperature possible.

Poached Chicken in Cream Sauce

(InspiredbyPierreFraney) and (Van Coppernolle, 2006)

Ingredients for 2 Servings:

- Protein Chicken Breasts boneless, skinless 2.

- Poaching Liquid Chicken broth low sodium 2 cup, or enough to submerge the chicken breasts.

  Bay leaf 1

Shallot 1 with two cloves

Allspice ground 1/8 tsp

Carrot, small two cut across.

Celery stalks two trimmed cut across 6-inch segments.

Kosher salt to taste.

Peppercorns 3

Thyme 1 sprig or ¼ tsp dried.

- Side dish   Rice 1 cup prepared as in parboiling, and steaming.

Garlic 3 cloves pressed.

Kosher salt one three-finger pinch.

Canola oil 1 Tbsp

1 ½ cup of the poaching liquid when done.

- Sauce   Cream sauce, a derivative of Bechamel sauce.

Ghee 1 Tbsp

Flour 1 tbsp

Poaching liquid ½ cup.

Heavy cream ½ cup

Lemon Juice of half a lemon

Freshly ground black pepper

Ground nutmeg in 1 two-finger pinch.

Ají amarillo powder one two-finger pinch.

Procedure:

1. Poach the chicken in a saucepan. Add the poaching liquid ingredients to the chicken breasts in a single layer. Bring to a boil, then reduce the heat to a slow simmer, covered. Simmer for 20 minutes to bring the chicken's internal temperature to 160°F. Remove from the heat.

2. Prepare the rice as in *Cooking Rice,* I am using the poaching liquid instead of water.

3. Meanwhile, make the cream sauce. Prepare a white roux with the butter and flour, whisking continuously; when homogenous, add the poaching liquid ½ cup, whisking rapidly, then add the heavy cream. Simmer for about 10 minutes; add salt and remaining sauce ingredients.

4. To serve, arrange the hot rice on a serving plate and cut the carrots and celery into 2-inch segments. Place the chicken over the rice and the vegetables, spoon the sauce, and serve.

Grouper poached with cream sauce

CHAPTER 8

Wet Indirect Heat

Double Steaming

Double steaming, sometimes called *double boiling*, is a Chinese cooking technique[1] to prepare delicate food such as bird's nest soup[2] and shark fin soup.[3] Cover the food with water and put it in a covered ceramic jar. Then, heat the jar for several hours in another pan with water. By doing this, the maximal temperature for the outer container is 212°F or 100°C (boiling water temperature) and will be steady at that temperature if there is water in the outside container. The temperature in the inner container will never exceed that temperature and will be lower because of the ceramic container's insulating effect.

Recipe for Bird's Nest Soup

The preparation of Bird's Nest Soup (Wikipedia, 2021) may use traditional methods, where the prep of the birth's nest is

---

(Wikipedia, 2021)
Wikipedia, "Edible Bird's Nest," accessed date March 25 2023,
https://en.wikipedia.org/wiki/Edible_bird%27s_nest

very labor intensive and can take an entire day. On the other hand, there is a product called Simply Swift Bird's Nest.

This product requires no prep work (by the user) and can be prepared quickly in 15 minutes. It may be cooked in the microwave or on the stovetop.

Bird's Nest Soup Microwave Preparation

1. Pour one cup of water into a microwave-safe bowl, at least a 4-cup size bowl (to avoid spillage).

2. Add one piece of Simply Swift and microwave on high for 4 minutes without cover. While still hot, add sugar, spices, or fruits for a sweet soup or other ingredients of your preference.

Bird's Nest Soup Stovetop Preparation
Egg and Ginger Bird's Nest soup

Ingredients for two servings

- Two pieces of Simply Swift

- 2 cups chicken stock

- one egg white

- 1 Tbsp soy Sauce

- 2 Tbsp of cooking rice vinegar

- two thin slices of ginger

- 1 tsp of Tapioca starch (yucca flour)

Procedure:

1. Pour the chicken stock birth nests, rice cooking vinegar, ginger, and soy sauce in a small saucepan.

2. Bring to a boil and then simmer for 15 minutes.

3. Remove ginger. Make a tapioca slurry with cold broth or water.

4. Add the slurry to the simmering soup and allow it to boil briefly to thicken.

5. Back to simmering, add the egg white while stirring constantly so the egg will not clump.

6. Garnish with diced ham and scallions.

7. Serve hot.

If the ingredients become overcooked, the bird's nest will lose its gelatinous consistency; therefore, you must pay close attention. An alternate method is the double steaming technique. In this method, you cook the soup inside a recipient (a tempered and transparent pickling bottle) in a Bain Marie. This way, the boiling water will not affect the preparation, and the temperature will be a constant 212°F 100°C of the Bain Marie reduced by the walls of the pickling bottle.

Bain Marie

The BAIN-MARIE is a cooking utensil containing heated water. It is used to cook food in a small pot placed over the one with heated water.

This technique is often used to warm food during gatherings when food is served on buffets or at tables.

It is a cooking technique used to prepare delicate dishes like custards (Cream Brûlée, Catalan cream, Flan), melting chocolate, and sauces, particularly those containing egg yolks.

Catalan Cream (unknown, /terra-cotta-crema-catalana-dessert)

Ingredients for six servings:

- 2-inch vanilla beam or 1 tsp of vanilla extract

- Whole milk 1 cup

- Heavy cream 1 cup.

- Cinnamon stick 1

- Zest of 1 lemon

- Zest of 1 orange

- Egg yolks 6

- Corn starch 1 Tbsp

- ¾ cups of sugar

Procedure:

1. In a double boiler, bring one inch of water to a boil. Place milk, cream, cinnamon stick, vanilla bean, and zests (lemon and orange) in the top bowl. Bring to a simmer for 2-3 minutes. Discard cinnamon and vanilla beans.

2. In a separate bowl, whisk the egg yolks with the cornstarch and 3/4 cup of sugar until incorporated and creamy. Slowly add this mixture into the warm milk, mixing continuously. Tempering the egg yolks mixture is always safer.

3. Slowly heat the mixture on the double boiler, stirring the entire time, until it begins to thicken. Do not boil. Pour into 12 shallow serving dishes, cool to room temperature, and refrigerate for several hours.

4. To serve, sprinkle cold custards with the remaining sugar and caramelize them with a torch or under a hot broiler.

Hollandaise Sauce

Ingredients for 2-3 servings:

- 1 Egg yolk

- 8.33 g. Water (1 Tbsp)

- 5 g. Lemon juice 1 Tbsp)

- 83.33 g. Clarified butter @ 165°F (5 Tbsp + 1 ½ tsp)

- Salt 1.3 g. (1 ½ tsp)

Procedure:

1. In a Bain Marie, add one egg yolk and water to the bowl to start (you may need more to maintain the emulsion).

2. Place the bowl on top of the saucepan with boiling water. Whisk continuously, rotating the bowl and lifting the whisk every so often to release the vapor and heat accumulated under the bowl. Continue this until you get a fluffy consistency and form a ribbon pale in color when lifting the whisk.

3. Remove from the heat and start adding the juice of a ½ lightly pressed lemon. Slowly drizzle the clarified butter. Add water and reheat as needed until you get the desired consistency.

4. Taste and add salt and lemon juice to taste.

5. Maintain warm steadily for up to 2-3 hrs.

Steaming (Smith, 2023)

It is a wet cooking method where the food product is not in contact with the boiling water; the vapor brings the energy in the form of heat carried to the food product. Vaporization begins at 100°F; vapor carries extra energy because of the change of state (from liquid to gas) that requires additional power in the form of heat, called the ***latent heat of vaporization***. Injuries from vapor are worse than boiling water because when in contact with skin, for example, it will liberate that extra energy to become a liquid, which is boiling water, so there is a double injury first from the change of state to liquid and a second from the hot liquid.

Since vaporization begins at 100°F and the temperature continues to increase until boiling occurs when it becomes stable, it is best to wait for the boiling to be present before placing the food product in the steamer. This way, you can accurately determine the cooking time at a constant temperature.

Steaming is best for food products with delicate structures, like fish, crustaceans, eggs, and vegetables. The cooking times for these products will be in the recipes.

The equipment is simple. A pot and a steam basket will suffice to steam anything.

Steaming Broccoli

- Bring one inch of water to a boil.

- Add a steamer Basket to the pot.

- Place the Broccoli florets on the steamer Basket and reduce the heat to medium to keep the boil.

- Add the lid and steam for 5-6 minutes.

The key to perfectly steamed vegetables is the steaming time, which is crucial so that the vegetables retain their crunch and do not become overcooked and soggy.

Recommended steaming times for some of the many vegetables are as follows: Asparagus 7-12 minutes, Brussels sprouts 8-12 minutes, Broccoli 5-6 minutes, Cabbage 5-10 minutes, Cauliflower 4-6 minutes, Carrots 8-12 minutes, Eggplant 8-10 minutes, green beans 6-8 minutes, mushrooms 4-5 minutes, Peppers 2-4 minutes, Spinach 3-5 minutes, and Zucchini 3-6 minutes.

***Stemmed Whole Fish with Ginger, Scallions, and Soy Sauce
Inspired by (Leung, 2023)***

Ingredients for two servings:

- Protein   2 Black Sea Bass 1 ½ lb. each.

- Fat   Canola oil ½ cup.

- Aromatics   Ginger 2 ½ segment, peeled and grated.

  Scallion 1 stalk white and light parts only, julienned.

  Rice wine 1 Tbsp

  Light soy sauce ¼ cup.

  Cilantro sprigs 4

- Seasoning   Sea salt and freshly ground black pepper.

Procedure:

1. Scale the fish and rinse in cold tap water. If previously frozen, soak for 10 minutes in a bath of salted water, about the same as seawater. ***Sea water has about 3.3 grams of salt per 100 ml. or about 3 Tbsp per liter (1 Tbsp = 13.8 g.),*** or about one tbs per 333 ml of water. Rinse in freshwater and pad it dry with paper towels.

2. I prefer, at this point, to remove the dorsal fin; it contains little bones (part of the rays or fin bones), which will be

removed with the dorsal fin. Cut the skin parallel to the dorsal fin on both sides, join the slits at both ends. Pull the dorsal fin from the tail end towards the head. The fin will come out with the dorsal rays' bones attached.

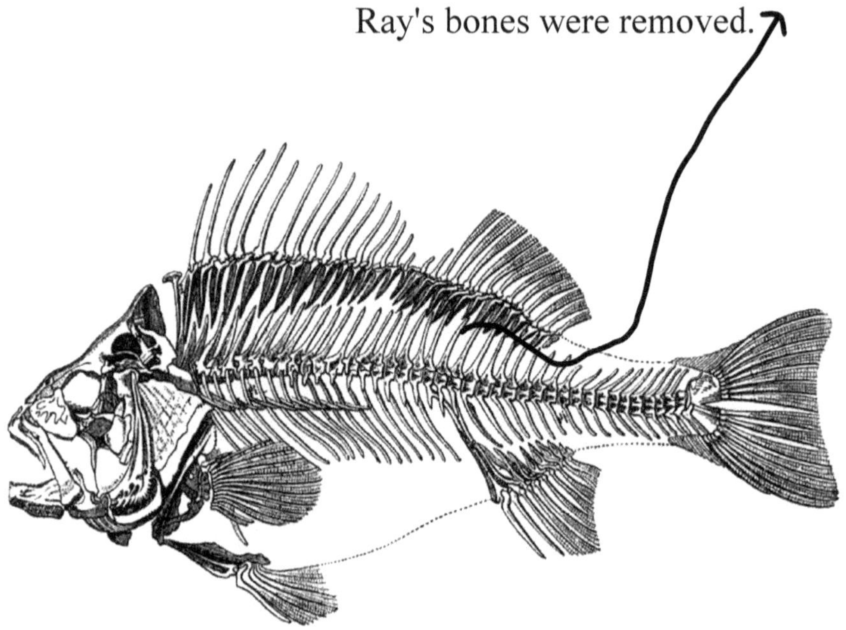

3. Place the fish in a heat-proof dish large enough to accommodate the fish and small enough to fit in the steamer. You may bend the fish to accommodate it in the dish if it is too long.

4. Put 2 inches of water in the bottom of a wok and set the steamer in it. Bring the water to a boil over high heat.

5. Place the fish in the dish in the steamer, cover, and steam for about 8 minutes until the fish flakes with ease when evaluated with the tip of a knife.

6. While the fish is cooking, mix the soy sauce with the rice wine and a Tbsp of water and set aside.

7. Remove the plate from the steamer, drain any fluid accumulated, and lay the cilantro sprigs and scallions over the top of the fish, where the dorsal fin used to be.

8. Heat the canola oil in a saucepan. When hot, pour over the scallion and the cilantro. Drizzle the soy mixture over the fish and serve.

Steaming Lobster Tails
(Mainlobstertailsnow)

Ingredients for 2-6 servings:

- Lobster tails 2-6

- Butter 1 Tbsp per tail

- Sea Salt 2 oz

Procedure:

1. The pot should have a tight-closing lid and be large enough to hold the lobster tails without overcrowding.

2. The lobster should be placed in a steamer basket that fits an upside-down colander; the lobster should be placed on top without touching the boiling water.

3. Pour in 2-inch of cold tap water. Cover the pot and bring the water to a boil. Once boiling, place the lobster tails, close the lid, and begin boiling according to the weight of the average tail. From 3 to 10 oz average one minute per oz; if they are more significant than an average tail, about ¼ of a minute per oz

4. Once you have reached the cooking time, check the center of the visible meat; expect it to be thoroughly cooked.

5. If so, stop them from further cooking by placing them in ice momentarily. Use tongues or gloves not to burn your hands; remember, steam is hotter than boiling water.

6. Serve them with melted butter.

CHAPTER 9

Fat Based High Heat Method

Introduction

Extra Virgin Olive Oil is recommended in most recipes involving frying. In the past, arguments against that practice have been made because of its low smoking point.

Swati Bhardwaj (EffectofheatingonTransfatacid) studied the formation of trans fats by heating and reheating fats or oils as used in Asian Indian cuisine. A similar practice is present in the USA in fast food restaurants, such as in the fryers for French Fried potatoes or Deep-Fried Chicken, where the oils will be changed weekly or at longer intervals.

Swati Bhardwaj studied six different oils and solid fats heated to temperatures between 180°-220°C 350-425°F; all of them showed an increase of trans fatty acids, an increase of saturated fatty acids, and a decrease of unsaturated fatty acids. All these changes would be unhealthy, with an increased risk for cardiovascular diseases.

A couple of years later (2018), another study was published in the Acta Scientific Nutritional Health (EVOO ok for Frying), where the concept of Oxidative Stability is given supremacy over smoking points. Their data (Dc Alzaa F, Guillaume C, Ravetti L.) shows that heating several oils to 240°C, 464°F

117

(Pan frying) and 180°C, 356°F (deep frier temp). Extra virgin olive oil ranks the best in Oxidative Stability, followed by coconut and avocado oils.

In conclusion, using Extra virgin olive oil for frying, sauteing, etc., is a desirable choice; frequent food intake at Fast-Food restaurants where oils are not changed often may not be a viable choice.

SGI Southern Green Industry, a company that recycles oils, makes these recommendations:

- Oil in a deep fryer lasts longer than in a skillet.

- Use oils with a high smoking point; they are more stable when cooking foods in high heat.

- The best high-smoking temperature oils include canola, sunflower, peanut, and avocado.

- Change the oil filter of the fryer of French Fries or non-breaded vegetables every 6-8 uses. If nonbreaded meat or poultry, every 3-4 uses. If breaded fish every 2-3 uses.

Those recommendations are aimed at commercial places, such as for the home user Kenny Lopez-Alt. (Lopez Alt., 2023) He has a publication with recommendations that include oil freshness and its ability to fry. These factors affect the qualities of an oil, such as the type of frying vessel, the type of coating of the food product, the type of food being fried, the kind of oil and temperatures being used, and the storage used.

Daniel Gritzer (Gritzer, Cooking with olive oil, 2023) from Seriouseats.com also reported on his experience using olive oil for high-temperature frying, concluding that there are no significant differences in the fumes of oils used at high temperatures. If large amounts of oil are used, like in an electric fryer, one should consider the flavor impact on the dish and the cost.

The research literature also supports the effect of thermal abuse of cooking oils on the facilitation of breast tumor spread to the lung in murine animal models. This is another reason to avoid degraded oils.

Recipes of High Heat Fat-Based Dishes

Even though grilled steaks are a favorite during warm weather, during wintry weather days, pan-frying, sauteing, stir-frying, or pan-searing and basting will produce great-tasting steaks.

Entrecote or Steak-Frites **Inspired by (Hill, 2022)**

Ingredients for four servings:

For the steak

- Protein Hanger steaks 2, separate each of the two halves, cutting the connective tissue in between. Cut off excess fat and silver skin.

- Fat Olive oil one tsp+

- Aromatics Shallots minced 2 Tbsp

- Liquid White wine dry ¼ cup

  Beef stock ½ cup reduced to half (1/4 cup).

For Sauce

- Protein   Anchovies fillets, two preferably white anchovies from the Cantabrian Sea.

- Fat   Butter, unsalted 3 Tbsp

- Aromatics   Parsley, fresh minced 1 Tbsp

                      Fresh Chervil, minced 1 Tbsp

                      Thyme, fresh minced 1 Tbsp

Procedure:

1. Sauté the steaks (pan hot, then oil hot), flipping once, until they reach an internal temperature of 125°F, 3-4 minutes on the first side, slightly shorter on the second side. Remove the steaks from the pan and cover them under tented foil.

2. Place shallots in the pan, back to the burner, and cook until they soften and become translucent; add wine and deglaze the pan by scraping the bottom of the pan to loosen the fond. Add broth and anchovy fillets and cook until thickened to sauce consistency. Remove from the heat, add the butter a bit at a time while whisking continuously, add the aromatics, and blend the contents of the skillet with an immersion blender.

3. Serve the steaks sliced in a slant, with sauce on top. French-fried potatoes or vegetables may accompany them.

Notes:

1. You may prepare a different sauce with balsamic vinegar, 2 tsp Butter unsalted, 2 Tbsp, and salt to taste.

2. May accompany with Potatoes Maxim type (CreamyAuGratinPotatoes)

Hanger Steak with Bagna Cáuda Inspired by(Gritzer, 2018) and (Gritzer, how-to-make-bagna-cauda-anchovy-pan-sauce-for-steak, 2018)

Ingredients for four servings:

- Protein   Two hunger steaks. Separate the hunger steaks into two parts, cutting the Connective tissue in between. Remove excess fat and silver skin.

- Seasoning   Kosher salt and freshly ground black pepper.

- Fat   Extra Virgin Olive Oil 2 Tbsp

For the Bagna Cáuda

- Fat   Extra Virgin Olive oil 3 Tbsp

  Butter unsalted 4 Tbsp cubed, cold.

- Protein   Anchovies, white from the Cantabria

sea, chopped.

- Aromatics   8 large cloves pressed.

  Ají Amarillo paste 1 tsp

  Lime Juice 2 Tbsp or juice from 1 fruit.

- Garnish   Cilantro leaves chopped ¼ cup.

Procedure:

1. Sauté the steaks, pan hot, then oil hot, flipping once. To an internal temperature of 125°F, 3-4 minutes on the first side (color change at the edge 2/3 up), slightly shorter on the second side. Remove steaks from the pan and cover them with tented foil.

2. Lower the heat to medium-low. Add the three tsp of olive oil to the same pan, stir in the garlic and anchovies (mashed into a paste with a fork), and cook until the garlic is lightly golden and the anchovies have dissolved into the sauce. Then add the ají Amarillo, then the butter, and stir until melted; stir lime juice, and remove from the heat.

3. Return the steaks to the same pan and baste them with the sauce.

4. Slice the steaks in a slant across the grain, serve immediately, and spoon the remaining sauce on top. Garnish with the chopped cilantro leaves.

Notes:

- You may make different sauces:

1. Beef demi-glaze made by reducing beef stock (store-bought) could strengthen the flavor by adding a beef base like "better than bouillon," a small coffee spoon, and shitake mushrooms.

2. A pan sauce based on balsamic vinegar (2 tsp), cold butter in cubes 2 tbsp), and salt to taste. (panSauce)

3. Or an Asian spice sauce based on Thai sweet chili sauce, soy sauce, and kecap manis (sweet soy sauce) or soy sauce, honey, and garlic.

- May be accompanied by roasted potatoes and roasted vegetables, steamed vegetables, or rice sushi cakes. (Lauren, 2023)

These recipes above all use hanger steaks, but of course, there are other cuts of beef meat, pork, fish, shellfish, or any thin product to be thoroughly cooked with sauteing technique. Thicker cuts will need an associated technique to cook the center portion without charring the surfaces, like simmering, basting, and roasting. Another alternative is using an electric grille, which I use adhering to those guidelines. Thin cuts ½ - inch or so 7 minutes each side uncovered, set at 360°F, internal temperature 120°F for removal from the grill, will get to 125°F while resting for 10 minutes.

Thicker cuts up to 1 ½—inch: 8 minutes on each side, set at 360°F, covered to an internal temperature of 120°F, remove from grill, and rest for 10 minutes.

For thin and thick cuts, reduce beef stock to ½ volume for a sauce, add one espresso coffee tsp of "beef base better than bouillon, or similar," and slice shitake mushrooms thickly.

Examples:

Pan fried Skirt Steak Inspired by (Franey, 1993)

Ingredients for four servings:

- Protein   Skirt steaks lean, trimmed 4.

- Seasoning   Kosher salt and freshly ground black

                       pepper to taste.

- Fat   Olive oil or vegetable oil 1-2 tsp

                       Unsalted butter 4 Tbsp

- Aromatics   Shallots cubed small ¼ cup.

                       Garlic pressed four cloves.

                       Thyme leaves fresh 1 tsp

- Flavorings/Acid   Red wine Vinegar 1 Tbsp

- Garnishing   Parsley chopped 4 Tbsp

Procedure: From skillet to a platter.

1. Trim excess fat from steaks.

2. Heat the skillet over high heat, large enough to hold the steaks in a single layer. Brush it with oil.

3. Brown each side of the steak until a nice crust has formed (about 3 minutes on each side). Remove from the skillet to a platter and cover with tented foil to keep warm and moist.

4. Discard any residual oil. Place ½ of the butter in the skillet, melt it, and add the aromatics. Cook until translucent. Add vinegar, heat it, and the remaining butter and parsley. Stir, and return the meat to the skillet. Turn the heat off and serve immediately.

Notes:

- Instead of shallots, you may use white onions, fennel, or other tubers.

- May be accompanied by French fried potatoes, roasted potatoes, pasta, or rice.

Pork Chops Asian Style (unknown, Food-and-dinning-cooking-&-recipes-cooking-meat-pork)

Ingredients for four servings:

- Protein — Pork Chops 4

- Aromatics — Teriyaki sauce 1 cup

  Garlic 4 cloves pressed.

- Seasonings — Kosher salt and freshly ground black pepper to taste.

  Light on the salt.

- Fat — Extra Virgin olive oil or olive oil cooking spray 1 ½ Tbsp or four sec. spray.

Procedure:

1. Marinate the Pork chops in half of the teriyaki sauce in a plastic, resealable bag in the refrigerator for at least 30

minutes or, if you desire, overnight since the marinade is not acidic.

2. remove the pork chops and shake off the excess marinade when ready to cook. Then, discard the marinade in the bag.

3. Heat a large, heavy skillet on high heat. Add the oil and, when shimmering, add the pork chops. Brown them on both sides. Add the reserved fresh marinade, lower the heat to medium, and simmer until the internal temperature reaches 145°F.

4. Serve after resting the pork chops for 10 minutes. You may accompany them with roasted potatoes or French fries.

Sauté Salmon with Asian Style Coleslaw Salad

Prepare the salad and the dressing first.

Ingredients for four servings:

For the Salmon:

- Protein   Salmon fillets, center cut four.

- Fat   Olive oil 2 Tbsp

- Seasonings   Kosher salt, freshly ground black pepper to taste.

Procedure for the Sauté Salmon:

1. Season the salmon fillets with salt and pepper and let them rest.

2. When ready, heat a large, heavy skillet on medium heat and add oil until shimmering. Rise the heat to medium-high, add the fish skin side up, and cook until golden brown on the bottom side, about 4-5 minutes, and the sides appear cooked about ½ the way up. Flip the fish over with a spatula, and cook the second side until the internal temperature reaches 125°F.

3. Remove the fish and serve with the dressed salad.

Asian Slaw Salad

Ingredients for eight servings

- 3 cups green cabbage or Chinese cabbage shredded.

- 3 cups red cabbage shredded.

- 2 large carrots julienned.

- 3 cups bean sprouts

- three green onions finely sliced and slanted.

- 1/2 cup coriander/cilantro leaves

- 1/2 cup mint leaves

- 1/4 cup Fried Shallots (optional) to garnish

Procedure for the salad:

1. Combine the salad ingredients, except the Asian Fried Shallots.

2. Pour over the dressing and toss to combine.

3. Garnish with Asian Fried Shallots. Serve!

Asian style Dressing:

Ingredients for 8servings:

- Fish or Lobster demi-glaze   5 Tbsp
- Rice vinegar   3 Tbsp
- Mirin   2 Tbsp
- Ponzu   3 Tbsp
- Fish Sauce Thai   2 tsp
- Ají Amarillo paste   1 Tsp
- Extra virgin olive oil or Rice Bran oil 3 Tbsp

Procedure:

1. Mix all ingredients but the oil in a medium bowl and whisk them to mix until the right thickness develops to your taste. Add the oil in a thin stream while whisking continuously.

Note: You may use other fish filets like groupers, snappers, or flounder.

Shrimp Stir Fry

Ingredients for four servings:

- Protein   1 lb. raw shrimp

For the Marinade

- 1 ½ tablespoons garlic, minced.

- two teaspoons ginger, minced.

- ½ teaspoon ají amarillo powder or crushed red pepper

- one tablespoon olive oil

- ⅓ cup honey

- ⅓ cup soy sauce

Garnish

- scallion, thinly sliced.

Preparation:

1. Place the peeled shrimp in a sealable bag or medium bowl.

2. In a small bowl or measuring cup, mix marinade ingredients.

3. Pour half of the marinade on the shrimp. Save the other half for later.

4. Let the shrimp marinate in the refrigerator for at least 15 minutes; it may marinate longer (no acid in marinade).

5. Pat the shrimp dry in paper towels.

6. Heat oil in a medium pan. Add shrimp to the pan, but discard the marinated mixture. Cook the shrimp on one side for about a minute, then flip over.

7. Pour in the remaining marinade and cook until the shrimp is cooked through and just firm. Remove the shrimp from the pan and reduce the marinade to make a sauce.

8. Serve the shrimp with sauce and garnish with green onion.

9. May accompany it with white rice or pasta.

Chicken Stir Fry Inspired by (Welch, 2024)

Ingredients for four servings:

- Protein   Skinless, boneless chicken breasts cut in 1-inch cubes 1 lb.

- Fat   1 and 1/3 Tbsp olive oil or olive oil cooking spray.

- Produce   Carrots, peeled, thinly sliced 1 cup, may use parsnips instead.

  Broccoli florets 2 cups

- Aromatics   Garlic 4 cloves pressed.

  Onion red cubed small one small.

- Seasoning and flavorings:

  Freshly ground black pepper to taste.

  Soy sauce ¼ cup

  Salt after tasing if needed.

  Honey 3 Tbsp

- Thickening agent   Corn starch slurry 2 Tbsp (1 Tbsp Each water and cornstarch)

Procedure:

1. Season the chicken with salt and pepper. Heat a heavy skillet on the stove. When hot, add 1 ½ tsp of oil or four sec. Spray.

2. Add broccoli and carrots and cook until tender, about 4 minutes. Remove the vegetables from the pan and keep warm with tented foil.

3. Wipe the pan, reheat high heat, and add the remaining oil. When shimmering, add the chicken in a single layer; do not overcrowd (to avoid steaming). You may need to do this in batches. Cook until golden brown, 3-4 minutes on each side. Meanwhile, in a small bowl, mix the soy sauce, chicken broth, and honey.

4. Add the garlic and cook for 20-30 seconds, then add the vegetables to warm them. Then add the sauce mix to the skillet and cook for another 30 seconds. Then, progressively add the cornstarch slurry and bring it to a boil to the desired thickness.

5. Serve immediately with rice or noodles.

Chicken Stir Fry

Thick Steaks Pan Cooked Inspired by (Lopez-Alt, 2017)

Kenji Lopez-Alt describes this method as replacing grilling when the weather changes or does not permit outdoor grilling. Recommends the use of a cast Iron skillet because of the superior heat-retaining characteristics of this pan, allowing a superior crust formation that enhances the flavor of the steak proper, developing a good contrast between the crust in the surfaces and the tender internal meat. The steak should be at least 1 ½ - inch thick.

Ingredients for 2-3 servings:

- Protein   T-bone or Porterhouse or Prime rib

- Fat   Canola oil ¼ cup

132

	Unsalted butter 3 Tbsp; may also use clarified butter.
• Seasoning	Salt and freshly ground Black Pepper
	(Seasoning done early and refrigerated).
• Aromatics	Rosemary or thyme six sprigs
	Shallots finely sliced one large.
	Ají Amarillo paste 1 tsp

Procedure:

1. Pat the steak dry with paper towels. Season with salt and black pepper for at least 45 minutes or overnight, if desired.

2. Heat the cast iron skillet large enough for the steak at hand. Once hot, add the oil and heat it until shimmering.

3. Add the steak. You may flip it as often as you desire, which helps cook it more evenly.

4. Add butter, herbs, and shallots. Continue to flip the steak occasionally and baste with the butter, concentrating on light spots of the crust. This permits the meat to cook faster. Keep basting continuously until done.

5. Control the heat source to avoid burning the butter or charring the crust. Continue this way until the internal temperature reaches 120°F. Remove the steak, pour the pan juice, and rest for 10 minutes. The internal temperature will rise to a safe temperature for consumption.

Slow roasted, Twice Fried Porterhouse Steak Inspired by (Talbot, 2015)

The website Bon Appetite.com published this method by Alexander Talbot and Kamosawa. It is labor intensive and involves prolonged preparation, but they promise it is worth it. They inspired me.

Ingredients for four servings:

- Protein   Porterhouse bone-in, 2-inch thick, marbleized.

- Fat   Vegetable oil about 4 cups.

  Unsalted butter or clarified 4 Tbsp

- For the Rub   Kosher Salt, 1 Tbsp

  Brown sugar 1 Tbsp

  Ají Amarillo Powder ½ tsp

- Flavoring   Masala curry powder 1 tsp

Procedure:

1. Mix the ingredients of the rub in a small bowl and set aside.

2. Prepare the steak by scoring diagonally about ¼ - inch deep and 1-inch apart.

3. Rub all sides of the porterhouse. Upend vertically on the flat of the porterhouse bone on a wire rack sitting on a baking sheet with elevated borders. Refrigerate

overnight (12 hours) and freeze for 6 hours minimum and up to 24 hrs. The purpose is to dry the meat surfaces to get a good crust.

4. preheat the oven to 200°F to soften the steak when ready to cook.

5. Prepare a cast iron skillet, heat it, and then add oil to about 3/4 inch enough to reach halfway the thickness of the steak. When shimmering, the oil temperature is 350°F, and the steak is soft enough to insert the temperature probe, add the steak directly from the freezer to the skillet. Cook for 3 minutes on each side. It should be deeply browned and have formed a crisp crust on each side.

6. Transfer the steak to the wire rack and roast in the oven until it is no longer frozen, about 30-35 minutes. Meanwhile, melt the butter in a small saucepan, then add the curry masala and mix. Remove from the heat, let cool, and strain through a fine mesh sieve into a small bowl.

7. Remove the steak from the oven, pour 1/3 of the butter mix over the steak, and brush it.

8. Return the steak to the oven and roast it for 1 ½ hours, basting with the remaining butter mixture every 30 minutes until the internal temperature reaches 120°F.

9. Remove the steak from the oven and reheat the skillet and its contents to 350°F over medium-high heat. Put the steak back in the skillet and fry it for 2 minutes per side and edges.

10. Transfer to the wire rack to rest for 10 minutes.

11. Carve the strip and the loin parts, slice them to the desired thickness, reconstruct the steak for presentation on a serving platter, and pour the juices from the baking sheet on top.

12. Serve immediately.

Steak au Poivre. Inspired by (Gritzer, Serious Eats, 2023)

Ingredients for two servings:

- Protein mignon

  Medallion steaks two like filet

  or hanger steaks cut as medallions.

- Fat

  Oil vegetable 1 ½ Tbsp

  Butter unsalted 1 Tbsp

- Seasoning

  Black Peppercorns 1 oz divided

  Kosher salt to taste.

- Aromatics

  Thyme 2 sprigs

  Garlic 1 large clove halved.

  Shallot 1 large, cubed small.

  Dijon mustard 1 tsp

  Ají Amarillo paste 1 tsp

- Liquid

  Brandy 2 Tbsp

  Chicken broth ½ cup

  Heavy cream ½ cup, or 4 Tbsp cream fraiche.

Procedure:

1. Preparatory steps: season steaks with salt on both sides and refrigerate in a wire rack.

2. Place peppercorns in a plastic bag and mallet them coarsely. Preheat oven to 375°F.

3. Spread the crushed peppercorns in a dish and press one side of the steaks on them.

4. Heat a cast iron skillet, add oil, cook until shimmering. Add steaks, peppercorns side down, and cook until peppercorns are toasted, about 3-4 minutes Carefully turn the steaks so as not to disturb the peppercorn crust.

5. Add the butter, thyme, and garlic, basting. Cook until the internal temperature of the steaks reaches 125°F for medium rare. By then, the second side will be well-seared. If you prefer further doneness, place the steaks in the oven to complete the cooking.

6. Pour all but 1 Tbsp Of the skillet's fat; discard the thyme and garlic. Add shallots and remaining peppercorns and return to medium heat; cook until shallots are translucent and tender. Add the brandy and cook until the alcohol has evaporated. Add chicken stock/broth to a simmer, scraping the fond. Add the heavy cream while whisking, add the Dijon mustard, and whisk it until it is dissolved. Continue to simmer until the sauce covers the back of the spoon and leave a finger strip.

7. Serve in a sauce bed, with steaks on top to display the toasted peppercorn crust. Accompany with French Fries.

Shrimp Tempura

Inspired by (John, 2023)

Ingredients for three servings:

- Protein   Shrimp large, 12 deveined dried in refrigerator uncovered.
- Fat   Canola oil for frier, according to manual instructions.

For the batter:

- ¼ cup all-purpose flour
- 1 tsp of baking powder
- ½ tsp Kosher salt
- ¼ cup of potato starch
- one three-finger pinch of Ají amarillo powder
- ½ cup of cold sparkling water

For the dipping sauce:

- ½ cup of lobster broth
- ¼ cup white wine
- ¼ cup of Ponzu
- one three-finger pinch of sugar or granulated stevia.
- Garnish with grated Jicama.

Procedure:

1. Make shallow cuts in the ventral surface to prevent curling when frying.

2. Pre-heat oil in the frier to 375°F

3. Mix all the dry batter ingredients in a bowl and whisk them, then add the cold sparkling water, continuing to whisk until smooth and homogeneous. Mix the dipping sauce ingredients in another small bowl, whisk them, and sprinkle with the grated jicama.

4. Coat the shrimp with the batter and fry about six at a time, separating them gently so they don't stick to each other until golden brown (3 minutes or so).

5. Serve shrimp with dipping sauce.

CHAPTER 10

Gentle Frying, Sweating.

Gentle Frying and sweating are methods that use low heat to allow the ingredients to cook primarily in their juices, but as with all frying, some oil is also used.

Gentle frying is used for the aromatic vegetable base in many recipes and may appear with names such as mirepoix, trilogy, aderezo, sofrito, and others. This method often requires that the vegetables be cut to about the same or proportionate size so they will cook at about the same time. It uses medium-low heat to avoid browning or caramelizing the vegetables.

Sweating uses medium-low heat, some oil, or cooking spray. It is used for sweating vegetables, fish, shellfish, and chicken. You aim to avoid browning or caramelizing the vegetables while preserving each ingredient's distinct flavor. You will often sweat the protein and aromatics simultaneously, and the juices of the protein and the vegetables will meld in unique flavors.

Sweating Vegetables

Sweated Onions, Carrots, and Fennel
Ingredients for four servings:

- Onion 1 red medium sliced thick.

- Carrots 2 medium, peeled cut in 2-inch-long batons ¼ inch thick.

- Fennel 1-bulb cut in slices across and then quartered.

- Thyme or cilantro, two sprigs.

- Butter 2 Tbsp

- Garlic pressed one large clove.

- Ají amarillo paste ½ tsp

Procedure:

1. Melt the butter at medium-low heat, add the vegetables, and cover them with parchment paper.

2. Check the progress closely; they can burn quickly. Remove the cover, stir to ensure even cooking, and allow sweat to evaporate. Cover them to keep the vegetables moist.

3. The vegetables will be cooked when tender, and the onions translucent; add garlic and Ají amarillo.

Sweating Proteins

Sweated Chicken

When sweating proteins, you may have to add vegetables to let fluids out or add liquid ingredients.

Ingredients for four servings:

- Protein   Four chicken thighs and legs, skinless and

boneless. Four.

- Aromatics   Tomatoes, Sliced thick, 2-3 depending on size.

  Onions, white, sliced thickly.

  Ají amarillo paste 1 tbsp

  Cilantro leaves chopped, 2 tbsp

- Fat   Olive oil 2 tbsp

  Unsalted butter or ghee, 2 Tbsp

- Green peas   Frozen, ½ cup

- Liquids   White wine dry ½ cup

  Chicken demi-glaze ½ cup

Procedure:

1. Sear the chicken to golden in a Dutch oven with hot oil.

2. Set the chicken aside on a plate and reserve it. Turn the heat to medium-low, add the onions, and cook until tender. Add the garlic, ají amarillo, and white wine, and reduce the white wine ultimately. Make a bed for the chicken with the tomatoes at the center. Add the chicken demi-glaze, heat to a simmer, and the reserved chicken over the tomatoes.

3. Add the green peas when the chicken's internal temperature is ready. If the sauce is not thick enough, bring it to a boil and add a cornstarch slurry (equal parts

cornstarch and cold tap water) slowly until the additions do not thicken the sauce anymore.

4. Serve over hot rice with the vegetables and sauce.

Sweated Skate Wings Inspired by (Flay, 2022)

Ingredients for four servings:

- Protein   1 two-pound skate wing, divided in 4 pieces.

- Fat   Canola oils: 2 Tbsp of Canola oil Spray, 4 second spray.

- Aromatics   Panca chili paste.

   Habanero chili 1 – sliced seeds and ribs removed.

   Onions red four sliced medium.

   Tomatoes concasse 3

   Bay leaf 1

   Cilantro chopped two tablespoons.

- Liquid   White wine ½ cup.

   Fish stock 1 cup.

Procedure:

1. Heat the oil in a large skillet until shimmering. Add the garlic and sauté for 3 seconds. Add the ají paste and cook for about 4 minutes until thickened and fragrant.

2. Add the white wine, bring to a simmer, and cook until reduced by half. Add the fish stock and simmer for 3-4 minutes so some reduction occurs and flavors meld together.

3. Add the onions, bay leaf, and tomatoes, and simmer for 5 minutes. The onions will start to become translucent but still crunchy.

4. Add the skate pieces to the pan, cover, and simmer for about 8 minutes. The internal temperature should be 115°F, but by the time you serve, it will be 125°F.

5. Ladle the soup into shallow bowls, garnish with cilantro leaves, and add some cooked rice if desired.

Sweated Grouper

Ingredients for four servings:

- Protein   Grouper filets 4- 6oz each.

- Carbohydrates   Fingerling potatoes 12 count

- Fat   Canola oil 2 Tbsp

- Aromatics   2 Red onions sliced medium.

  Tomato concasse of 2 tomatoes.

  Tomatoes sliced medium 2.

  Habanero chili is sliced finely, seedless, and deveined.

  Cilantro 4 sprigs + 2 tbsp of leaves chopped.

- Liquid   White wine dry ½ cup.

                         Fish stock ½ cup.

                         Juice of 2 Key West limes.

- Seasoning   Sea Salt and freshly ground black
  pepper.

Procedure:

1. Parboil the potatoes.

2. Heat the canola oil in a skillet large enough to hold all ingredients.

3. Sauté the onions and the concasse of tomatoes until the onions start becoming translucent. Add the white wine, cook off the alcohol, and reduce by half or more. Add the fish stock, the grouper, habanero, cilantro sprigs, and potatoes, and cover the fish with the sliced tomatoes. Cover the pan and lower the heat to simmer for 8 minutes.

4. Check the internal temperature of the fish; check the potatoes with the tip of a knife will be done if the potato's resistance is minimal and the fish's internal temperature is 115 F.

5. Season with sea salt and pepper to taste.

6. Serve in a large shallow bowl. Garnish with the chopped cilantro leaves.

Sweated Grouper with tomato sauce and roasted potatoes

Sweated Shrimp Inspired by (Acurio, PERU, 2015)

Ingredients for four servings:

- Protein   Shrimps 40 cleaned and deveined.

- Aromatics   Onions red, medium, three sliced

- Fat   Olive oil 2 Tbsp

     Garlic 4 large cloves Pressed.

     Ají Amarillo paste 2 tsp

     Tomatoes are sliced thick and seedless.

     Cilantro 4 sprigs.

     White wine ½ cup

     Fish stock, reduced by half ½ cup (demi-glaze)

- Seasoning Salt and freshly ground Black Pepper.

Procedure:

1. Place the shrimp in a large saucer with the onions, garlic, and 1 tsp of Ají amarillo and cook for 2 minutes over medium heat.

2. Add the wine, fish demi-glaze, the remainder of the ají paste, and tomatoes, cover, and cook until the shrimp is done and pink and the temperature is 125°F.

3. Arrange the shrimp, vegetables, and sauce in a serving bowl and garnish with the cilantro leaves.

CHAPTER 11

Braising, Guisos, Etouffee, Estofados, Stews.

These combination methods usually involve quick sautéing at a high temperature of the dish's protein being prepared to develop the Maynard reaction on the surface of the protein of choice. You do not want to cook it thoroughly, so it is often reserved aside. In the same pan, at low heat, cook the aromatics of your choice (onions, garlic, chili paste, bell peppers, celery, and carrots, cubed small) slowly.

Then, add a liquid to simmer and cook the protein and vegetables appropriately. Depending on the liquid, the amount of liquid and the origin of the heat may receive different names. Some minor changes in the ingredients will also produce quite different dishes. If the liquid covers only partially the protein, then it is braised. It is stewing if the liquid covers the protein completely (usually cut in chunks).

They are accompanied by side dishes such as country bread slices, rice, mashed potatoes, parsnip puree, and roasted or fried potatoes, which usually absorb the sauce.

1. ***Estofado*** (stew, Fricassee—white stew-, seco) is done on the stovetop. First, sear the protein, then add the liquid so that it covers or is near covering the protein; if

meat, it usually is the tougher cuts with tendinous material that will soften when cooked in medium-low heat for extended periods. It may contain any combination of vegetables.

The method uses:

- The Maillard reaction, caramelization of surface sugars (320°-338°F)

- Deglazing the pan, previously used for searing, by adding a cold liquid.

- Simmering with reduction of the liquid to about ½ of the original.

- The proteins can be domestic meats (beef, chicken, duck, pork, or rabbit) or game meats equivalent to the domestic. They can also be fish, shellfish, or vegetables like cabbage, corn, potatoes, okra, often may need to have added fat to prevent scorching the vegetables (bacon, sausage, chorizo)

2. *Etouffee*: or smothering regional to the Cajun or Creole cuisines. Most often with shellfish, often crayfish, and uses stove top heat.

3. **Guisos** uses the same searing, simmering, and deglazing methods. The medium is semi-greasy, allowing the flavors of the oil, seasonings, and condiments to meld with the flavors of the protein and vegetables.

4. *Encebollados*: This is a variation of the stir fry from the Far East with a mixture of Peruvian cuisine. You stir fry the components separately so the pan will not be

crowded, avoiding the products being steamed. Begin with the protein (beef, fish, or shrimp), sometimes with a thickening agent (flour, corn starch), follow with the onions cut thickly, and add the aromatics like chili, garlic, bell pepper, and celery. Then, you add the liquid in a measured amount, often white wine vinegar; it brightens the ingredient flavors and sweetens them. They are usually accompanied by rice and French fries.

Stew of corvina

Braised Vegetables

Braised Leeks

Ingredients for 4-6 servings:

- Star Ingredient — Leeks long white shanks 4-6
- Carbohydrate — Sugar or granulated stevia 1 tsp
- Fat — Unsalted butter 3-4 Tbsp
- Aromatics — Garlic minced two large cloves.

  Thyme dry 1 tsp or fresh 2 tsp

  Bay leaf one.
- Garnish — Parsley, chopped ¼ cup.
- Simmering Liquid — White wine 1 cup.

Procedure:

Clean the leeks:

1. Cut the green of the leeks; we will be using only the white and a small light green portion.

2. Do not cut the roots yet. Split in half lengthwise, short of the root end.

3. Wash the leeks under running tap water, cold.

4. Cut the roots now, thus separating the halves.

Sauté the halved leeks in butter:

1. Melt the butter in a large skillet, large enough to hold the leeks in one layer. When the butter's foaming has subsided, turn the heat down to medium and add the garlic and the leeks cut side down. Cook a few minutes, turn them over, and repeat the process.

Simmer:

1. Turn the leaks to cut side down again. Sprinkle the leeks with sugar, thyme, and salt. Add the wine and bay leaf and bring to a gentle simmer. Cover and simmer for 30-45 minutes until the leeks are tender so you encounter no resistance when pierced with a paring knife tip.

2. Remove the leaks, bring the braising liquid to a boil, and reduce by half.

3. Serve with the sauce and garnish with the parsley.

Braised Fish

Corvina with Potatoes Guiso

A guiso is a combination method from Spanish origin and assimilated to most old Spanish colonies. Uses searing, simmering, and deglazing. The simmering liquid is a semi-greasy medium that melds oil, aromatics, spices, protein, and vegetables. The fish (corvina) is a Pacific coast fish with a habitat that extends from South America to the southern Pacific

Coast of the USA. The corvina fish meat is white, firm, and ideal for ceviche and slow-simmered guisos.

Ingredients for 6-8 servings:

- Protein — Corvina filet divided into 4-6 oz pieces (1 ½ lbs.).

- Carbohydrates — Potatoes, Russet 2 large, if small,

  One per serving, peeled and cubed.

- Fat — Extra Virgin olive oil 4 Tbsp

- Aromatics — Tomatoes, plump 3

  Onion red, medium cubed medium.

  Garlic 3 cloves pressed.

  Parsley chopped 2 tbsp

  Pimenton de la Vera 1 tsp

  Ají amarillo 2 tsp

- Seasoning — Kosher salt to taste.

- Water — 1 cup.

Procedure:

1. **Prep the base (sofrito):** Heat a broad skillet to accommodate all the ingredients. Add the oil and heat to the shimmer. Lower the heat to medium and add the onion, garlic, ají amarillo. Cook slowly until the onions are translucent. Then add the potatoes and continue to cook until they turn golden brown.

2. Remove the skillet from the heat source, add the pimentón (smoked paprika), and stir to incorporate in the mixture. Put back to the heat source. This maneuver is necessary to prevent the pimenton from burning.

3. **Add the liquids** (for the sauce)**:** Add the crushed tomatoes and the parsley, and cook for another 10 minutes, stirring. Add the water; when boiling, cover the skillet, lower the heat, and simmer for 15 minutes.

4. **Add the protein:** Add the corvina pieces in a single layer as much as possible. Simmer for 5 minutes, then turn the heat off. Rest the whole preparation for five more minutes before serving. The sauce is delicious. You may accompany the dish with rice or country bread to soak up the sauce.

Braised corvina with Puttanesca sauce

Simmered Mangrove Snapper Japanese style.

Ingredients for two servings:

- Protein   1 ½ lb. Mangrove Snapper

- Ginger root   peeled and cut in batons 1 ½ inch long by ¼ inch thick.
- Burdock root   12-inch segment split lengthwise in 8.

For simmering liquid:

- Water   1 ½ cups.
- Sake   ½ cup.
- Mirin   3 Tbsp
- Sugar   3 Tbsp
- Soy sauce   4 Tbsp

Procedure:

1. Clean the fish (it should be gutted and the gills removed) and wash the cavity with cold tap water. For scaling, have two bowls large enough to contain the fish, one empty and one with ice water. Place the fish in the empty bowl, pour boiling water over them, and immediately transfer them to the ice water. Now, scale them quickly.

2. Mix all the simmering liquid ingredients in a large pot. Add the burdock root segments around the edges of the pot. Heat to a boil.

3. Meanwhile, make diagonal cuts along one side the length of the fish, about 1 inch apart, and stuff the ginger matchsticks on the top side only.

4. When the liquid is boiling, turn down the heat to simmer, add the fish with the diagonal cuts up, cover with parchment paper, lower into the pot to the surface of the

preparation, and simmer for 10 minutes. Uncover and baste the fish surface with the liquid, and cook until the sauce thickens or the fish's internal temperature reaches 125°F.

5. To plate, put the fish on a serving plate. Cut the burdock root into bite-size pieces and place them around the fish. Cook the sauce until thickened, then pour it over the fish on the serving plate.

Fresh Cod Escabeche

Ingredients for four servings:

- Protein   Fresh Cod 6 oz Filet four pieces, flour dusted on both sides.

  Hard Boiled Eggs 2 sliced.

- Carbohydrates   Sweet Potatoes, medium size, 4 sliced ¼ inch thick.

  Flour all-purpose ½ cup.

- Fat   Olive oil 4 Tbsp

- Aromatics   Red onions, medium size, thick slices, four onions.

  Garlic 3 cloves, pressed.

  Ají Amarillo, seedless, sliced 2 or 2 tsps. of Ají Amarillo paste.

  Mustard Dijon 1 tsp

Ají Panca paste 1 tsp

Ají Amarillo paste 1 tsp

- Seasoning agents   Kosher salt, freshly ground black

  Pepper to taste.

  Oregano leaves, chopped 2 tbsp

  Cumin ground 1 tsp

- Produce   Lettuce Boston or Little Gem,

  Four large leaves.

- Liquid   Red wine vinegar, ¼ cup.

- Garnish   Corn on the cob, boiled cut into
  round slices about 1-inch thick.

  Olives Black Alonso 8 halved.

Procedure:

Cook the fish.

1. Season the fish, dredge with flour, and shake the excess. Heat a skillet large enough for the fish to be in a single layer. Add a couple of Tbsp of oil and heat it to shimmering. Sauté the fish at medium heat, presentation side down, and cook until the edges change color to about halfway. Flip the fish; it should be golden brown on the top side. Cook the bottom side until the internal temperature reaches 125°F and the edges show cooked coloration. Remove from the pan and rest covered with foil.

Make the base and sauce.

2. Add the remaining oil, heat it, and then add the onions. Cook at medium heat. After a minute, add the garlic and ají amarillo strips seedless, the ají amarillo and ají panca pastes, the salt, pepper, and cumin. Cook, stirring for 3-4 minutes, to allow all flavors to meld. Then, add the vinegar and the oregano. Immediately turn off the heat.

3. Serve with a leaf of lettuce on the plate. Place the fish in the center of the leaf. Cover the fish with the onion sauce and garnish with the sweet potatoes, hard-boiled egg slices, olives, and corn cob segments.

Note: this dish may be served warm or at room temperature.

Fish Piccata Inspired by (Joann, 2013) (D'Arabian, n.d.)

Ingredients for four servings:

- Protein   White fleshed fish filets,

  thickness ½ to 3/4-inch, flounder, seabass, haddock, etc., four pieces of six ounces.

- Carbohydrates Flour all-purpose ½ cup.

- Fat   Vegetable oil 4 Tbsp divided.

  Unsalted butter 4 tbsp

  Unsalted butter 1 Tbsp worked into ¼ tsp of flour to a paste.

- Seasoning   Kosher salt and freshly ground black

  pepper to taste.

- Flavorings
1 ½ Tbsp of capers drained from vinegar.

Lemon Juice of one fruit.

Parsley chopped 2 Tbsp

Ají amarillo paste 2 tsp

- Liquid
White wine 1/3 of a cup.

Procedure:

Sauté the fish.

1. Season the fillets with salt and pepper to taste. Dredge them in flour, shake off the excess, and place them on a plate covered with parchment paper.

2. Heat a nonstick skillet at medium-high heat, add oil, and heat it to shimmering. Place the fish presentation side down in the skillet, in batches, if necessary, and cook until the edges change color to about ½ way up (3-4 minutes). Using two spatulas flip the fillets and cook the second side until internal temperature riches 125°F about less than a minute, depending on the thickness and type of the fish. Remove the fillets from the skillet, cover with foil to keep warm.

3. Wipe the skillet, return it to medium-high heat, add wine, heat it to a boil, and keep it at a simmer. All the alcohol smell should burn off, and the wine should be reduced to half. Add the 4 Tbsp of butter, the butter-flour mix, and the capers, and whisk continuously at a simmer until creamy. Add lemon juice and parsley, season with

salt and pepper, whisk, pour over the fish, and serve immediately.

4. If the sauce breaks (usually too much heat), add tap cold water one Tbsp at a time until the emulsion is re-established.

Braised Monk Fish

Ingredients for six servings:

- Protein   Monk Fish Tail 1 ½ lbs. or Halibut steak or fillet, swordfish.

- Fat   Olive oil extra virgin 3 Tbsp

- Carbohydrates   Potatoes, Idaho 1 lb. peeled and cut into 1-inch cubes.

- Aromatics   Onion red, large cubed medium size.

  Thyme sprigs two.

  Saffron 1 two-finger pinch.

  Ají Amarillo paste 1 tsp

  Carrots, medium cut in 1-inch chunks.

  Small size fennel bulb, cut about the same size as the carrot pieces.

  Tomato paste, 2 Tbsp

  Paprika smoked (pimentón)

- Liquid   Red wine dry ½ cup.

Chicken demi-glaze 2 ½ cups (Reduction by half of broth).

- Seasoning   Kosher salt and freshly ground black pepper.
- Garnish   Parsley chopped 3 Tbsp

Procedure:

Sear the fish for a Maillard reaction.

1. Heat a Dutch oven or heavy skillet; when hot, add olive oil and heat until shimmering. Season the fish with salt and pepper. Cook at medium-high heat until well browned (5-6 minutes); remove from the pan to a plate, browned side up, and cover with foil.

Prepare the base and sauce.

2. Add the first 6 Aromatics (onion, thyme, saffron, ají amarillo, carrots, fennel) and potatoes. Cook at medium heat, stirring until the onions soften (± 5 minutes). Add the tomato paste and continue to stir until the tomato paste darkens a little (± 3 minutes). Add the wine, scrape the fond from the bottom of the pan, and ultimately let the wine reduce.

Simmer.

3. Add the Chicken demi-glaze, reduce by one-third, and simmer for 10 minutes. Then, add the fish nestling among the vegetables, keeping the liquid below the browned surface of the fish (braising). Cook undisturbed for 10 minutes. Check the internal temperature of the fish. If it is 125°F, it's done; otherwise, allow it to reach the safe temperature for fish of 125°F.

Plate.

4. Transfer the fish to a cutting board and slice it into six 6-oz servings. Divide the vegetables between shallow bowls and place the fish portions over them. Season the simmering liquid and ladle it over the fish and vegetables. Garnish with parsley.

Fish and Shellfish Stew (Peruvian Parihuela)

Ingredients for four servings:

- Protein   Monk Tail, a large one

  Grouper filet 4 pieces

  Shrimp, large 4.

  Mussels 1 dozen

  Calamari, baby size 8

- Carbohydrates   Flour, all-purpose

- Fat   Olive oil, extra virgin.

- Aromatics   Onion red, large, cubed small.

  Garlic clove, large, pressed.

  Bell Pepper, small, seedless, one cubed small.

  Tomatoes concasse, 3

  Ají Amarillo paste 1 tsp

  Saffron 1 pinch.

- Deglazing liquid Brandy 2 Tbsp

- Seasoning — Kosher Salt and freshly ground black pepper to taste.
- Flavoring — Almonds 2-3 Tbsp
- Simmering liquid — Fish stock or broth 1 cup (may use the shrimp shells to make a broth)
- Garnish — Parsley fresh, chopped 2 Tbsp

Preparation of ingredients:

- Remove the fish bone from the tail of the Monk Fish. Cut the tail across into four pieces.

- Clean the shrimp, shelled and deveined. Save the shells for the broth.

- In a pot, cook the mussels in ¼ inches of water until the shells open. When ready, remove them, strain the water, and save it for the broth. When they have cooled enough to handle, remove the shells and barbs and set them aside.

- Dust the grouper filets with flour and sauté them in the olive oil, just enough to brown the surfaces.

- Clean the baby calamari, cut the tentacles from the body, and remove the contents. Sauté the tentacles and body fully so they won't be rubbery. Reserve them.

Procedure:

1. In a large heavy pot or Dutch oven, heat 3-4 Tbsp of olive oil on medium-low heat. When shimmering, add onions, sweet peppers, and garlic. Sauté until they soften.

2. Cut the almonds into cubes and dry roast them in a small skillet (if the almonds are not peeled, blanch them and peel them first).

3. Toast the saffron lightly and prepare croutons.

4. Mix saffron, almonds, croutons, and parsley in a mortar and pestle. Crush as much as possible.

5. Add the fish, shrimp, and calamari to the Dutch oven when the sofrito is soft and ready. Deglaze the bottom with the brandy and allow the alcohol to evaporate.

6. Add the fish or shrimp broth and some mussels' broth from cooking the mussels. (Add enough for evaporation in the next 10-15 minutes).

7. Add the almond mixture, stir, and cook for 4-5 minutes to meld the flavors.

8. Serve hot.

Braised and caramelized Grouper

Ingredients for two servings:

- Protein   Grouper 6 oz Filet pieces.

- Washing solution   If fish frozen and thawed

  4 Tbsp Kosher salt per liter of tap water.

- Fat   Olive oil 2 Tbsp

- Aromatics   Garlic 5 cloves large pressed.

  Onion red medium sliced thick.

  Ginger root 1-inch peeled and grated.

- Braising liquid   Fish sauce 1 ½ Tbsp

Ponzu sauce 1 Tbsp

Coconut water 1 cup.

- Seasoning   Freshly ground black pepper.

- Garnish   Green onion chopped in a slant.

  Slices of seedless, veins removed, red or yellow chili.

Procedure:

1. Prep the washing solution by dissolving the salt in water. Soak the fish in it for 10 minutes and then rinse with cold tap water. Dry with paper towels and set aside, uncovered to dry.

2. Heat a heavy nonstick skillet. Add one tbsp of oil and heat it to shimmer. Add the fish and sauté until golden brown on both surfaces. Set aside on a platter.

3. Add the remaining oil to the same skillet, add the onions, and cook them on medium-low heat until translucent. About halfway through, add the garlic and stir to avoid burning it.

4. Add the braising liquids, turn the heat up, and boil the liquid. Lower the heat to simmer, add the fish, and simmer partially covered to the fish's internal temperature of 125°F. Remove from heat.

5. Garnish with green onions and black pepper, and serve fish in the center, onions on top, and braising fluid over.

Grouper and Shrimp with Maracuya (Passion Fruit), Honey, Mustard Dressing

Ingredients for two servings:

For the sauce

2 Tbsp Oil, avocado, or canola

- 1 cup of Maracuja concentrate juice.

- Honey 2 Tbsp

- Mustard Dijon 3 Tbsp or honey mustard

- Garlic minced two cloves.

- Ginger finely minced 1 tsp

- Heavy cream or coconut milk 1 cup.

- one onion sliced thin (sautéed with the garlic and ginger before mixing

For the oven or grill

- 4- 6 oz portions of filets of grouper, thick.

- 6-8 shrimp peeled, deveined tail on or off your preference.

Procedure:

- Preheat the oven to 425°F.

- Sauté onions, add ají amarillo and garlic.

- Mix all other sauce ingredients in a small bowl and add the onion mix.

- Place a serving of grouper fillet and 3- 4 shrimp in the center of aluminum foil. Pour some of the sauce on top. Wrap it all in aluminum foil for baking or grilling.

- Do the same with the second serving. Ensure enough sauce is left to pour over the dish after cooking.

- Bake for about 10-12 minutes (5' per lb.) and measure the temperature of the thickest serving for an internal temperature of 125-130°F.

- Let it rest in the foil wrap for 5 minutes, and add the additional sauce.

- Serve with rice or mashed potatoes.

Notes:

1. You may prepare this dish with chicken instead of fish. Sauté the chicken to brown the surface and finish in the oven with sauce, etc. Add corn grains and green peas to fish or chicken in the oven packet.

2. You may use tamarillo sauce using tamarillo pulp. Tamarillo, or tree tomato, is an edible egg-shaped fruit with a tart flavor. The recipe for the sauce follows.

Ají and Tamarillo Sauce:

Ingredients:

- 2 Tbsp vegetable oil

- 3 Tbsp ají amarillo paste.

- one small white onion diced small.

- two garlic cloves minced or pressed.

- 6 Tamarillo fruit or 6 Tbsp of Tamarillo pure

- ½ cup olive oil, salt and pepper to taste.

Procedure:

1. Sauté the ají amarillo until it curdles (3'); add the onion and garlic sequentially and sauté until translucent (3-5 '). Turn off the heat.

2. If using Tamarillo pulp, mix it with the sauté onion mix and olive oil in a blender, season with salt and pepper, and mix to your taste. If using the fruits, prepare concasse and proceed as above.

   Use by Adding to an already cooked protein or simmering a seared protein in the sauce.

Fish with Peperonata (Lata, 2019)

Peperonata is an Italian side dish. It uses Bell peppers, red onions, and multiple aromatics, including crushed tomatoes, garlic, and herbs. It can be prepared a day or two in advance to accompany grilled or golden-browned fish braised in the Peperonata sauce during warm months.

The choice of fish is yours. It works best with firm, white-fleshed fish such as haddock, corvina, grouper, amberjack, swordfish, flounder, halibut, etc. The cooking method for the fish is your choice: grilled or browned and then braised in the sauce to 125°F.

Ingredients for four servings:

- Protein   Fish of your choice 1 ½ lb. skinned, boneless.

- Fat   Olive Oil extra virgin, 4 Tbsp Divided.

- Seasoning   Kosher salt and freshly ground black pepper.

- Aromatics   Garlic 4 cloves pressed.

  Onion red sliced thick, lengthwise.

  Ají Amarillo paste 2 tsp

  Bell Peppers thinly sliced 8 cups (±2 lb.)

  Tomatoes crushed 1 ½ cup.

  Capers rinsed, 2 tbsp

  Oregano dry ½ tsp

  Thyme dry ½ tsp

  Paprika smoked 1 tsp

- Liquid   White wine, champagne, or rice

vinegar 2 Tbsp

- Garnish   Cilantro leaves chopped 2 Tbsp

Fennel thinly sliced, ¼ cup.

Procedure:

Brown the fish.

1. Brush oil and Salt and pepper the fish portions, rest on a plate.

2. Heat a large, heavy skillet or saucier, add 2 tbsp of olive oil, and heat to shimmer at medium-high heat. Then add the fish portions to the skillet and cook till golden brown, about 2 minutes; flip the fish carefully and brown the other side. Remove from the skillet and set aside.

Prepare peperonata.

3. On the same skillet, lower the heat to medium-low, and add garlic and ají paste, stirring often to prevent the garlic from burning, for a minute or 1 ½ minutes. Add the crushed tomatoes and cook for 4-5 minutes; add then the oregano and thyme, stir, remove the skillet from the fire, and add paprika while off the heat (paprika will burn quickly and give a bitter taste), stir, and bring skillet back to the heat. Add bell peppers, reduce the heat to low, and cook for about 15 minutes, maintaining a slow simmer. Add then the onion and cook for five more minutes. Add capers and return the fish to the skillet, nesting it between the peppers. Taste if acidic enough; if not, add vinegar progressively while tasting to a taste of

your liking. Cook for the fish's internal temperature to reach 125°F.

4. Plate the fish in the center. Spoon the peperonata over the fish and around it. Garnish with cilantro and fennel.

5. May accompany the dish with fettuccine and use the peperonata as a pasta sauce.

Fish Stew

Ingredients for four servings:

- Protein — White firm-fleshed fish like grouper, Corvina, porgy, cod, haddock. 1-2 lbs. in chunks. May add shellfish like scallops, mussels, shrimp, lobster, etc.
- Fat — Olive oil 2 Tbsp

  Sour cream ¼ cup.

- Aromatics — Onion white, medium cubed large

  Garlic 2 cloves large pressed

  Tomatoes diced 15 oz can.

  Tomato-paste 2 Tbsp

  Bell pepper is red, green, and yellow, one of each sliced and seedless.

  Ají amarillo paste 2 tsp

  Coconut milk ½ cup.

- Garnish — Cilantro leaves chopped 2 Tbsp

Procedure:

Prepare the Fish.

1. If the fish has been previously frozen and thawed, soak it for 10 minutes in salted water (3.3g salt per 100cc of water), rinse it in cold water, and dry it with paper towels.

2. Brush the surfaces of the fish with olive oil. Season with salt and pepper; let them rest for a few minutes,

3. Sauté them for the Maillard reaction. Put them aside, covered with a foil tent.

Prepare the stew sauce.

1. Heat a large, heavy skillet or saucer; when hot, add oil and heat to shimmer. Then, add the onions. When softening, add garlic and stir. Add diced tomatoes, tomato paste, coconut milk, and sour cream. Stir and simmer for a few minutes to meld all flavors.

2. Add bell peppers and reserved fish of your choice, taste, and season to your liking. Simmer for 10-12 minutes (may vary depending on the type of fish) so the fish flakes easily. Ensure the fish is submerged in the sauce; otherwise, turn it over or add some fish stock.

3. Serve in a shallow bowl over rice (pilaf style).*Example recipe* Rice Pilaf method

Braising Shellfish

Shrimp or Crawfish in Coconut Sauce. Inspired by (Merano, 2018)

Ingredients for six servings:

- Protein   Shrimp 21-25/lb. Count, 2 lbs.

  Or crawfish 40 tails.

  Shell removed and deveined.

- Fat   Coconut milk (regular)

  14 fluid oz 2 Cans.

  Unsalted butter 2 Tbsp

- Carbohydrates   Flour all-purpose 2 Tbsp

Corn starch 2 tsp

- Aromatic   Onion red, medium, cubed small.

  Ají amarillo paste 2 tsp

  Chopped cilantro leaves 2 Tbsp

- Seasoning   Kosher Salt 1 tsp or to taste.

- Flavorings   Aromatic Pisco or brandy 2 Tbsp

Procedure:

Prepare the sauce.

1. Heat a large saucepan and melt the butter over medium heat. Add the onion and ají and cook until translucent but not brown. Stir in the pisco or brandy and reduce the alcohol altogether.

2. Add the flour and mix quickly. Add the coconut milk, lower the heat, and simmer low and slow for about 10 minutes to blend all flavors.

3. Remove from the heat, cool some, put the mixture in a blender, blend thoroughly, and strain through a fine sieve. Discard the solids. Add the cornstarch to the strained coconut mixture, stir, and rest for 5 minutes.

4. Heat the strained coconut mixture in a saucepan and simmer for ten additional minutes; the sauce should be thick enough to cover the back of a spoon and leave a track when swiped with a fingertip.

5. Add the shrimp and simmer for 2-3 minutes; correct the seasoning to your taste.

6. Serve over rice (pilaf style) and garnish with the chopped cilantro leaves.

Mongolian Shrimp and Broccoli
Recipe inspired by (Shepherd, 2017)

Ingredients for four servings:

For the sauce:

- Soy sauce ½ cup.

- Sesame seed oil 1 Tbsp

- Brown sugar ¼ cup. You may use Kecap Manis instead of soy sauce and brown sugar 2/3 cup.

- Garlic pressed 3 tsp

- Ginger grated 2 tsp

- Chicken broth ¾ cup

- Ají amarillo paste 1 tsp

- Oyster sauce 1 Tbsp

For the dish:

- Protein — Shrimp peeled and deveined 8 oz

- Carbohydrates — Corn Starch 3 Tbsp

- Fat olive oil extra virgin 2 Tbsp

- Seasoning — Kosher salt and freshly ground black pepper.

- Aromatics — Bell pepper, seedless and deveined, One finely sliced.

Green onions are sliced in a slant of three stalks.

- Produce — Broccoli 1 large head, cut in florets.

- Side dish — Pasta of your choice or rice.

  Konjac Noodles fettuccini style, sauté, 16 oz (Skinny®) for low-carb diets. Optional 4 Tbsp of bean sprouts and two scallions in ½ inch segments.

Procedure:

For the Sauce

1. Mix all the sauce ingredients in a small bowl, then set aside.

For the dish

2. Season the shrimp with salt and black pepper. Set Aside.

3. Heat a large skillet or a heavy saucer at medium-high heat. When hot, add 1 Tbsp of oil and sauté the shrimp until pink. Flip them so all sides are pink (do not overcook); set aside.

4. Add the remaining olive oil to the same skillet. When hot, lower the heat to medium. Add the bell peppers and broccoli and cook until tender.

5. Then add the cooked shrimp and the sauce pre-mixed ingredients and continue to cook. Prepare a corn starch slurry by adding the same amount of cold water to the corn starch. Dissolve, add progressively to the sauce in the skillet, and bring the mixture to a boil to thicken.

6. Depending on your choice, boil the pasta or prepare the rice, pilaf style **Example recipe *Rice Pilaf method***

7. Open the packages of the konjac noodles, strain them in a colander, and wash them with cold water. Let them drain for several minutes. Add 1 Tbsp of the oil in a separate skillet, sauté the Konjac fettuccine in the hot oil, and add 1 Tbsp of ponzu, green onions, and beansprouts.

8. Plate a bed of fettuccini in the center and spoon the shrimp, broccoli, and sauce over it.

Picantes or Ajíes

In Peruvian cuisine, a group of dishes is called Picantes (spicy hot) or ajíes (chilies). They are prepared using a combined method involving searing the protein and then braising or stewing the aromatics to finish cooking it. It is a very savory dish, and the degree of spiciness flavoring is entirely up to you. Ají is spicy and has a flavor of its own, which adds umami to the dish.

You can also choose the protein used. It is often done with fish, shrimp, other shellfish like scallops, a medley of shellfish, or poultry like chicken.

Shrimp Picante

Ingredients for six servings:

- Protein   Shrimp count 12-16/lb. two pounds
- Carbohydrates   White bread, fresh crustless, or whole wheat.
- Fat   Unsalted butter 2 Tbsp

- Aromatics

    Half and Half 1 cup

    Gruyere cheese grated ½ cup.

    Onion red, large, cubed medium one.

    Garlic 3 cloves pressed.

    Ají amarillo or habanero slices, seedless 6.

    Ají Panca paste 1 tsp

    Walnuts 3 oz chopped into small pieces.

- Seasoning

    Black Pepper freshly ground.

- Flavorings

    Cumin ground 1 tsp

    Shio Koji seasoning 2 tsp

- Liquid

    White wine dry 2 Tbsp

Procedure:

1. Clean the shrimp, shelled and deveined. Brush the Shio Koji over the shrimp. If available, make a shrimp stock with the peel and heads, reducing to your liking.

2. Soak the bread in half and Half, add walnuts, and reserve.

3. Sauté in butter the shrimp until they turn pink; remove from the pan and reserve.

4. In the same skillet sauté, the aromatics and seasonings. Add the reserved stock and the milk and bread-walnut mixture.

5. Simmer for 5-7 minutes to meld all the flavors.

6. May serve as an appetizer or a main course with rice or pasta.

Note: you can use the same recipe and change the protein to scallops, fish, or chicken.

Curried Mussels.
Inspired by (Roland, 2018)

Ingredients for six servings:

- Protein   Mussels 5 Lb.

- Fat   4 Tbsp olive oil, extra virgin

- Aromatics   Shallots medium, diced medium.

  Lemon grass two stalks.

  Ginger 2-inch peeled and grated.

  Curry Madras paste 5 oz

- Simmering, deglazing   Madeira or Marsala wine 2 Tbsp

  Coconut cream three cans 14 oz each.

  Fish sauce 2 Tbsp

  Palm sugar 1 Tbsp

  Lime juice of 1 fruit.

  ½ tsp Kosher salt

		Unsalted butter, one stick of 4 oz
•	Garnish	6 limes halved and grilled.

Procedure:

1. Heat a Dutch oven large enough to fit mussels.

2. Add oil over medium heat. Add aromatics and cook for 2 minutes; do not brown.

3. Deglaze with the wine and burn off the alcohol.

4. Add one can of coconut cream, whisking to avoid burning at the bottom.

5. Add the remaining coconut cream, fish sauce, and palm sugar and simmer for 20 minutes. Strain the mixture and discard the solids. Place the strained liquid in the Dutch oven.

6. Add the mussels, butter, and salt, cover, and steam the mussels until they are open. Do not overcook.

7. Squeeze the lime juice and simmer for a minute.

8. Serve in a shallow bowl, top with the sauce, and garnish with the cilantro leaves and lime halves.

Shrimp butter.

Ingredients for four servings:

•	Protein	Shrimp peeled, deveined, ½ lb.
		cut in ¼ -inch segments.
•	Fat	Butter unsalted, 4+ Tbsp

- Aromatics   Shallots ¼ cup cubed small.

  Mace ½ tsp

  Ginger powder ½ tsp

  Nutmeg freshly grated one dash.

  Kosher Salt I pinch.

  Ají amarillo powder ½ tsp

- Liquid   Lime juice 1 tsp

  Sherry dry 3 Tbsp

Procedure:

1. Melt the butter in a skillet. When hot, add the shrimp and shallots and sprinkle the spices. Stir to coat the shrimp evenly. Cook for 1 minute and add the sherry. Cook until the shrimp is just done, and the alcohol has evaporated about 2- 3 minutes. Remove from the heat, add the lemon juice, check the seasoning, and correct if necessary.

2. Place in a blender and pulse 4-5 times until finely chopped but not a paste.

3. Place the skillet back on the heat, dissolve the remainder of the butter, and remove the skillet from the heat when the foaming stops. Add the shrimp mixture and stir. Transfer to a ramekin. If the butter does not cover the solids, add sufficient melted butter to do so. Refrigerate for at least 4 hours. It will last 3-4 weeks in the refrigerator.

4. Soften in an oven at 250°F for 1 hour before serving over crackers or Melba round toast.

Braising, Stewing Poultry.

Braised Chicken Thighs with Onions and Mushrooms. Inspired by (Candace, n.d.)

Ingredients for six servings:

For the dry rub:

- 1 tsp dry rosemary

- 1 tsp pimentón (smoked Paprika)

- 1 tsp coriander seed powder

- ½ tsp freshly ground black pepper

- ½ tsp ground allspice

- ½ tsp grated nutmeg

For the Chicken

- Protein   Chicken thighs skin on, boneless tied in a roll of skin wrapped around.

- Fat   Olive oil extra virgin

- Produce   Mushrooms Baby Bella 12 oz sliced thick.

Lime juice of ½ fruit.

- Carbohydrates   3 oz Dry figs halved or apricots.

- Aromatics   Shallots, peeled, halved 6.

Garlic cloves pressed 10.

Tomato Paste 4 tbsp

Mustard, Dijon 1 Tbsp

- Simmering liquid   Port wine ¾ cup.

  Chicken broth (low in sodium) and reduced by half 2 cups.

  Bay leaves 2 Rosemary dry, 1 tsp

- Garnish   Parsley fresh leaves, chopped 2 Tbsp

Procedure:

1. Preheat the oven to 350°F. Combine the dry rub ingredients in a small bowl. Prep the chicken by removing the bone, wrapping the meat with the skin, and tying it with twine. Rub the chicken thighs with the spice mixture and set aside.

2. heat 2 Tbsp of extra virgin olive oil in a large saucer or Dutch oven, covering all the bottom. If necessary, spray with olive oil spray, at medium-high heat. Once shimmering, add the chicken thighs and brown to golden brown. Cook undisturbed for about 6 minutes, flip, and repeat the process on the other side. Transfer the chicken to a plate, cover with foil, and set aside.

3. Add the shallots and garlic to the same pot; lower heat to medium and cook them until fragrant; add the tomato paste, Port wine, and mustard, and stir to a simmer for 3-4 minutes. Nest the chicken in the simmering liquid, ensuring it does not cover the chicken completely; the top of the skin should be dry. Transfer the skillet to the oven.

4. Measure the internal temperature of the thickest thigh. If it is below 165°F, roast it in the oven, cook uncovered, and check the temperature often. Depending on how cold the chicken was before browning, the time it will take for the internal temperature to reach 165°F will vary.

5. Meanwhile, sauté the mushrooms in olive oil until soft and cooked. When done, add to the chicken braise, and use the opportunity to check the chicken temperature; add more time as necessary.

6. When done, remove from the oven, finish with the lemon juice, and garnish with the parsley.

7. Often, braises are accompanied by rice or potatoes puree. Other alternatives are sweet potatoes, carrots, or parsnips puree. If you want a low-carb option, cauliflower rice, Pasta zero® fettuccini style, or Skinny Rice stir-fried are good options.

Estofado de Pollo/ Braised Chicken

This is a Peruvian-styled dish (guisos); even though stewed chicken is made in many South American countries and many other countries in the world, the Peruvian version is differentiated by using chilis, in this case for the Panca chili, a version of a dry chili (Capsicum Chinese) and the Ají amarillo that is mildly spicy hot but imparts a significant umami effect giving the dish an intense savory taste.

Ingredients for four servings:

- Protein   Chicken thighs, skin on deboned 4.

- Carbohydrates   Potatoes Idaho peeled and cubed large 2.
- Fat   Olive oil extra virgin 4 Tbsp
- Aromatics   Onion red, medium size, cubed medium one.

  Garlic pressed 1 Tbsp

  Tomato concasse cubed two large tomatoes.

  Carrots medium, cut in ¼ inch-thick rounds and then halved.

  Ají Panca Paste 1 tsp heaped.

  Ají amarillo Paste 1 tsp heaped.
- Seasoning   Kosher salt and freshly ground black pepper to taste.
- Flavoring   Cumin ground 1 tsp
- Produce   Green pees frozen ½ cup.
- Garnish   Cilantro leaves chopped 2 Tbsp
- Simmering liquid   Chicken broth low sodium 2 cups.

  Red wine 2 Tbsp

Procedure:

1. Remove the bone from the thighs. Wrap the skin around the meat and tie each thigh in a cylinder bundle. Season the chicken with salt and pepper to your taste.

2. Heat a large, heavy skillet. When hot, add the oil and decrease the heat to medium-low. When the oil shimmers, add the chicken thighs. Sear them to golden brown, turning them so all the skin is seared. When done, remove the chicken thighs, place them on a plate, cover with foil, and set aside.

3. Make the aderezo (base preparation, sofrito). In the same skillet and residual oil (if necessary, add more), add the onion, the ají amarillo paste, ají panca paste, and tomato concasse. When the aderezo is ready, add the chicken thighs and carrots. Add 2 cups of chicken broth, the wine, and a two-finger pinch of salt, cover, and cook at low heat for 30 minutes. Check at the 5-minute mark to see if the simmer is right (slow simmer).

4. Add the frozen green peas Five minutes before the 30-minute simmer. Take the opportunity to check whether the chicken's internal temperature has reached 165°F or more. Check the potatoes with the tip of a paring knife; they should give little resistance if they're done.

5. Remove from the heat, sprinkle the cilantro leaves, check the seasoning, and correct if necessary. Serve with rice pilaf, Peruvian style.

Estofado de Pollo-Braised Chicken

Chicken curry

Ingredients for two servings:

- Protein   3 chicken thighs, boneless and skinless

- Marinade   Juice of 1 lime

- Aromatics   1 Tsp minced garlic

  Ají Amarillo 1 tsp heaped.

  Red onion, cubed small.

- Fat   3 Tbsp Cooking olive oil is divided into three portions.

- Seasoning and flavoring: 1 Tbsp curry powder, Madras1 Tsp

  Tamarin fruit paste 1 Tsp

  Cube of cilantro paste 1.
  See note.

- Simmering liquid ¼ cup coconut milk

  ¼ cup coconut pulp shredded small

  ½ - 1 cup of chicken broth

Procedure:

1. Marinate the chicken in the lime juice for 10 minutes. Then sauté the chicken cut into strips just to brown. Place apart.
2. Prepare the sofrito in the same pan. Place 1 Tbsp of oil on medium heat, add onions, and cook for a minute or two. Add garlic and ají amarillo and cook for a couple more minutes.
3. Complete the Masala by adding all other ingredients (curry powder, tamarin fruit paste, cilantro paste, one Tbsp olive oil, coconut milk, chicken broth, coriander paste, and shredded coconut pulp). Cook for 5 minutes to thicken some.
4. Add the final tablespoon of olive oil and the chicken, and cook for another 4 minutes, stirring all along.
5. Serve over rice or boiled potatoes.

Note: Cilantro Paste recipe.

- 4 cups (packed) cilantro leaves (about a pound of coriander weighed with stems on)

- two cloves of peeled garlic.

- 1/2 cup unsweetened coconut milk

- 1/2 cup roasted peanuts.

- 1/4 cup fresh lime or lemon juice

- Salt

Procedure:

1. Rinse the cilantro well and pat dry.

2. Place the leaves, garlic, coconut milk, peanuts, and lime juice in a food processor. Process it into a fine puree and season with one teaspoon of salt or to taste.

3. Divide into an ice cube tray and freeze.

Chicken Fricassee Inspired by (Gore, 2023)

Fricassee is a stew made with pieces of meat cooked in butter and then served in a white sauce flavored with cooking stock.[2] Fricassee is usually made with chicken, veal, or rabbit, with variations limited only by the ingredients the cook has at hand.

It is a hybrid method combining a dry method (sautéing) and a wet method (stewing). A key difference in the sautéing part is that browning is avoided, so the meat is cooked using a gentle heat, avoiding the Maynard reactions of browning. The stewing part uses cream or coconut cream to obtain the creamy white sauce.

Ingredients for four servings:

For the sauté part

- Olive oil extra virgin 2 Tbsp
- Chicken thighs bone in and skin on 2 lb.
- Kosher salt and freshly ground black pepper to taste.

For the base

- Fat   Butter unsalted 2 Tbsp
- Carbohydrates   All-purpose flour 1 ½ Tbsp
- Aromatics   Onion red, large, cubed large 1(one).

  Carrot large cubed large 1(one).

  Celery cubed large one stalk.

  Mushrooms shitake sliced thick. 8 oz

  Ají Amarillo paste one heaped tsp
- Simmering liquid   White wine ½ cup.

  Chicken broth low sodium,

  reduced by half, 1 cup.

  Heavy cream 1 cup.

  Parsley chopped 2 Tbsp

  Thyme leaves, fresh, 2 Tbsp

Procedure:

1. Season the chicken on both sides with salt and pepper. Heat a heavy skillet over medium heat. When hot, add oil. Add the chicken thighs and cook partially when

shimmering, but don't brown. Then flip and cook the other side the same, about 5 minutes per side. Remove them from the skillet and set them aside on a platter.

2. Add the butter to the same skillet. Add the aromatics (onion, carrots, celery, mushrooms, and ají) when melted and still at medium heat. Cook until soft, about 5 minutes.

3. Add the flour (1 ½ Tbsp), cook for a minute, and then add the wine. Scrape the fat from the bottom of the skillet from cooking the chicken and burn the alcohol by reducing the wine by half.

4. Add broth and cream, parsley, thyme, salt, and pepper to taste. Add the chicken back to the skillet and simmer until the chicken's internal temperature reaches a safe temperature of 165°F. The sauce should have thickened to a **nappe**, be able to cover the back of a spoon, and leave a track when swiped with a fingertip (about 15 minutes).

Note: You may use the same recipe with alternate proteins, such as veal shoulder in chunks (or veal shank) or rabbit meat, to obtain equally good-tasting dishes. You can accompany them with rice pilaf style, sauté cauliflower rice with green onions, roast potatoes, or rustic bread to soak up the dish's star and the sauce.

*Simmered Chicken Asian Style **Inspired by (Food.com, n.d.)***

Easy to make and clean after.

Ingredients for four servings:

- Protein   Chicken Breasts, skin on 4

- Fat   Olive oil Extra Virgin 1½ Tbsp

Simmering liquid

- Liquids and aromatics   Soy Sauce 1/3 cup.

  Brown sugar 1/3 cup or

  Brown Stevia 1/3 cup.

  Water or chicken broth ½ cup.

  Ketchup 1 Tbsp

  Sherry dry ¼ cup.

  Ají amarillo paste 1 tsp heaped.

  Garlic clove 2 pressed.

  Green onions, white only sliced two stalks.

- Thickening agent   Cornstarch 2 tbsp mixed 1 Tbsp water

Procedure:

1. Heat a heavy, deep skillet or a Dutch oven under medium-high heat. When hot, add the virgin olive oil and heat it to shimmering. Add the chicken breasts and brown each side to golden brown.

2. Meanwhile, in a bowl, mix the soy sauce, brown sugar, chicken broth, ketchup, Ají amarillo, garlic, and green onion. Simmer for 10 minutes. Add the chicken to the sauce, cover, and simmer for 45 minutes.

3. Remove the chicken to a serving platter, add the cornstarch slurry to the sauce, bring to a brief boil, and diminish the heat while stirring. When the sauce has thickened, pour it over the chicken and the accompanying rice pilaf, Peruvian style.

Chicken Piccata Inspired by (Laurentiis, n.d.)

Ingredients for 4:

- Protein
  Two chicken breasts, skinless, boneless, butterflied, and cut in half crosswise.

- Carbohydrate
  All-purpose flour for dredging.

- Fat
  Unsalted butter 5 Tbsp
  Olive oil extra virgin, 6 Tbsp

- Aromatics
  Garlic 4 cloves, pressed.
  Shallots 2 chopped.

- Simmering Liquid
  Juice of 2 lemons
  Chicken stock reduced by half, ½ cup.
  Capers, rinsed ¼ cup.

- Garnish
  Parsley flat leaf, 1/3 chopped.

- Seasoning
  Kosher salt and freshly ground black pepper to taste.

Procedure:

1. Prep the chicken, season with salt and pepper, dredge in flour, and shake the excess.

2. Heat a large, heavy skillet on medium-high heat. When hot, add 3 tbsp of butter and 2 tbsp of olive oil and heat until they shimmer. Then add the chicken and sauté each side for about 3 minutes until golden. Flip them over and repeat. You may have to do it in batches. Remove them from the skillet and set them aside.

3. Lower the heat to medium, add more butter and oil, then add the shallots; when they soften, add the garlic and cook for a bit, not browning them. Add the juice of the lemons and scrape the fond, add the stock, bring to a boil, then lower the heat to a simmer, return the chicken to the skillet, and simmer for 5 minutes to the internal temperature of the chicken at 165°F. Remove the chicken to a serving platter. Add the remainder of the butter and whisk the sauce well. Pour the sauce over the chicken; if serving with pasta, save some of the sauce for the pasta.

Hunter Chicken Stew (Pollo alla Cacciatore).
Inspired by (Oliver, n.d.)

Ingredients for six servings:

- Protein   2 lb. Chicken or equivalent chicken pieces.

  Anchovies, preferably white, from the Sea of Cantabria.

- Carbohydrates   Flour for dusting the chicken.

- Fat   Extra virgin olive oil

- Aromatics   Tomatoes diced one can 14.5 oz or

  1 lb. tomato concasse.

  Tomato paste, 1 tbsp

  Onion, red, cubed medium 1 cup.

  Garlic 2 cloves, divided, pressed.

  Bay leaves 4

  Rosemary 2 sprigs

- Seasonings   Kosher salt and freshly ground

  black pepper to taste.

- Simmering liquid   Chianti wine 1 cup.

- Fruit   Black olives Alonso (Alfonso)

  or kalamata.

  Plums tinned one tin (±200g.)

Procedure:

1. Season the chicken or chicken pieces with salt and pepper and place them in a bowl. Add half the garlic, cover with the wine, and marinate overnight, preferably overnight.

2. When ready to cook, preheat the oven to 350°F.

3. Remove the chicken from the bowl and reserve the marinade. Dry the chicken with paper towels and dust it

with flour. Heat the oil in a heavy, oven-proof pan. When shimmering, sauté the chicken to brown it all over. Remove it from the pan and reserve.

4. Sauté the onions on medium heat until translucent. Add the remaining garlic and olive oil as needed. Add the diced tomatoes, the tomato paste, the anchovies, and the olives, then add the chicken and marinade. Bring to a boil, lower the heat to a simmer, and cover the pan with a lid or a double layer of foil. Transfer the pan to the oven and bake for 1 ½ hours.

5. Skim for any accumulated oil on the surface, remove the Bay leaves and Rosemary sprigs, correct the seasoning if necessary, and serve over rice or pasta.

Chicken Tagine Stew Inspired by
(ATK Cookbook)

This dish from Northern Africa is a stew rich in species, simplified somewhat by using products combining several spices.

Ingredients for two servings:

- Protein   Chicken breast boneless, skinless

  one of 8oz

- Carbohydrate   Flour all-purpose 1 Tbsp

  Chickpeas 1 can 14 oz rinsed.

- Fat   Olive oil extra

- Aromatics   Red Onion small, cubed medium

  Garlic cloves, two pressed.

Garam masala powder 1 tsp

Pimenton 1 tsp

Ají Amarillo paste 1 tsp

- Seasoning   Kosher salt, freshly ground black-pepper to taste.

- Simmering liquid   Chicken broth 2 cups.

  Tomatoes diced one can 14 oz

- Fruit   Dry apricots, quartered, ½ cup.

- Garnish   Cilantro leaves, minced 1 Tbsp

Procedure:

Cook the base (aderezo, sofrito, mirepoix)

1. Heat a heavy, medium-sized skillet. When hot, add oil. When shimmering, add the aromatics and ¼ tsp of salt. Cook at medium heat until onions are translucent (about 5 minutes). Stir in flour and cook for a minute.

2. Slowly whisk the broth and scrape the fond from the base preparation. Stir in tomatoes, chickpeas, and apricots. Season the chicken with salt and pepper and add it to the stew. Lower the heat to medium-low and simmer covered until chicken reaches 160°F (10-15 minutes). Flip the chicken about halfway.

3. Remove the chicken from the heat, transfer it to a board, and shred it with two forks to bite size. Return the chicken to the stew to reheat. Stir in cilantro and serve over rice pilaf.

Chicken Stew

It is a single-pot dinner, savory and delicious, enjoyable with country bread.

Ingredients for four servings:

- Protein   Chicken thighs, boneless, skinless, cut into 2-inch chunks.

- Carbohydrates   Flour or corn starch 2 Tbsp

  Baby white potatoes, 12

  oz quartered.

- Fat   Canola, avocado, or olive oil 1 Tbsp

- Seasoning   Kosher salt and freshly ground

  black pepper to taste.

- Aromatics   Carrots, medium 3, diagonally cut

  into ½ inch pieces 3.

  Red onion, cut into thick slices.

  Garlic, six cloves, pressed.

  Bay leaf 1

- Simmering liquid   Chicken stock, reduced by half,

  5 cups, divided.

- Garnish   Parsley flat leaf, chopped ¼ cup.

Procedure:

Brown the chicken.

1. Season the chicken with salt and pepper to taste—heat oil in a Dutch oven at medium-high heat. When shimmering, add the chicken chunks, stirring occasionally to brown all sides, about 5-6 minutes. The purpose is to brown the surface, not to cook the chicken. Transfer to a dish and set **aside.**

Prepare the base.

2. Lower the heat to medium-low, add the carrots and onion, and cook, stirring often, until the onions are translucent; do not brown. Then, add the chicken, the reduced chicken broth, the bay leaf, and seasonings. Bring to a boil, reduce heat to a simmer, and partially cover for 25 minutes.

3. Add the potatoes and cook uncovered until tender to a knife tip (18-20 minutes).

4. When the potatoes are ready, prepare cornstarch or flour slurry with 4 Tbsp of cold water. Drip the slurry into the stew, bring it to a boil, and add it progressively until the sauce no longer thickens. Discard the bay leaf before serving.

Braising Veal

Veal Marsala (Laurentis)

This dish is also a contribution of the Italian Immigrants to Perú, enriching the Peruvian cuisine.

Ingredients for four servings:

- Protein   Veal cutlets 3oz each, eight.

- Fat   Unsalted butter 3 Tbsp

                         Olive oil extra virgin 3 Tbsp

- Aromatics   Shallots, medium, two cubed small

                         Garlic cloves, medium 3 pressed

                         Rosemary leaves of 1 sprig

- Produce   Shitake Mushrooms, , 2 oz sliced.

- Simmering liquid   Marsala wine, sweet ½ cup.

                         Chicken broth, low salt, reduced by

                         half ¾ cup.

- Seasoning   Kosher salt, freshly ground

                         black pepper.

Procedure:

Season and sauté the veal cutlets.

1. Season the veal cutlets with salt and pepper.

2. In a heavy skillet, heat 1 Tbsp of butter and 1 Tbsp of olive oil; when shimmering, add four cutlets and cook to golden brown; flip them over and cook the second side, about 1-2 minutes per side. Remove the cutlets to a plate and repeat the process for the last four cutlets, including adding the butter and oil.

Prepare the base.

3. When the culets are done and set apart, lower the heat to medium-low, add 1 Tbsp of oil, and add the shallot and garlic when shimmering. Cook until fragrant (1/2 minute), then add the mushrooms, allowing the juices to evaporate and the mushrooms to be tender (± 3 minutes).

4. Add the wine and simmer for half (2 minutes). Add the chicken broth reduction and rosemary leaves and continue to simmer for half (± 4 minutes).

5. Return the cutlets to the skillet and the juices exuded on the plate. Cook to warm and flip them. Add another Tbsp of butter and season the sauce.

6. Serve, may be accompanied with rosemary roasted potatoes. (*Parboiled Roasted Potatoes*)

Veal Filets

Ingredients for six servings:

- Protein   Veal fillet cut from a whole loin,

  It should be thick, cut in an oblique, six pieces.

  Anchovies, white (Sea of Cantabria) Six filets.

  Ham French style six slices.

- Fat   Olive oil 2 Tbsp

  Unsalted butter 2 Tbsp

  Cheese of your preference (Munster) six slices.

- Carbohydrate   Flour for dusting.
- Aromatics   White onion, sliced thick across 6 slices.
- Simmering Liquid   Red wine, dry, 2/3 cup.
                        Veal demi glaze ½ cup
- Seasoning   Kosher salt and freshly ground black pepper to taste.

Procedure:

Sear the filets.

1. Season the filets with salt and pepper to taste. Sear them in equal parts of butter and oil to golden brown.

2. Add the wine and scrape the bottom to rescue the fond. Cook covered at a simmer; add the demi glaze progressively to soften and cook the meat some.

Set up for oven roasting at 350°F.

3. Place the filets in a greased baking pan and top them with onions, ham, and cheese. Top it all with anchovies mashed and mixed with one tsp of gastrique, a recipe to follow.

4. Roast the filets to an internal temperature of 125°F. Serve with broiled potatoes, small and white.

Gastrique recipe.

Ingredients:

- 4 tbsp granulated sugar. To avoid sugar, use 4 tbsp Stevia and 1 tsp molasses.

- 4 tbsp water

- 2 tbsp dry cranberries, diced.

- 2 ½ tbsp ruby port

- 1 ½ tbsp Balsamic vinegar

Procedure:

1. Prepare caramel by heating the mixture of water and sugar. Boil until it starts taking some color.

2. Remove from heat and add diced cranberries. Back on the heat.

3. Remove from the heat again and add port, back to the heat, and reduce until it reaches the napper stage (covers the back of a spoon and leaves a track when swiped with a fingertip. Then, it is ready to cool and use.

Veal in Bechamel Sauce.

This dish uses the same principles as the Fricassee method.

Ingredients for four servings:

- Protein   Veal loin or sirloin 2 Lb.

- Fat   Unsalted butter 2 Tbsp

                   Oil canola or avocado, to sauté- the

                   veal 2 Tbsp

- Carbohydrate   Flour 1 Tbsp

                   Potatoes white small 1 lb.

- Seasoning   Kosher salt and freshly ground

black pepper to taste.

- Aromatics   Carrots sliced in the oblique ½ -inch size.

  Bay leaves 2

  Oregano leaves minced 2 tbsp

- Produce   Mushrooms Shitake 2 oz

- Liquids   Whole milk 3 cups

  Beef broth reduced to half, 1 cup.

Procedure:

Sear the veal meat.

1. Wash and dry the veal meat, seasoning with salt and pepper to taste. Sear the meat to golden brown at high heat in a large, heavy skillet. Then add the reduced beef broth (1 cup), reduce the heat to a simmer, cover, and cook for 1 hour. Double-check the simmer after a few minutes. You may need to reduce the heat or use a "diffuser" to avoid excessive boiling.

Make the bechamel sauce.

2. In the meantime, make the bechamel sauce. Place the milk, carrots, bay leaves, and oregano in a saucepan. Bring to a gentle boil and cook to reduce the milk by one-third. Sieve and discard the solids. Keep the milk warm.

3. Melt the butter in another saucepan. When melted, add the flour progressively, stirring continuously to avoid lumps forming. Add the warm, flavored milk and continue to stir. If you wish, you may add Gruyere cheese to your taste.

4. Simultaneously boil the potatoes until minimal, but some resistance is felt when pricking with a paring knife. Mix the veal meat cut in slices with the bechamel sauce and serve with the sauce over it and the potatoes around.

Braising Pork.

Pork Tenderloin in Basil Sauce. Inspired by (Pakus, 2019)

Ingredients for four servings:

- Protein — Pork tenderloin whole.

- Fat — Light cream 1 ½ cup.

  Extra virgin olive oil ¼ cup.

- Aromatics — Pesto 4 Tbsp

  Garlic 2 cloves

  Pine nuts 50 g.

  Basil 1 bunch

  Parmesan cheese ½ cup.

Procedure:

Sear and simmer the pork tenderloin.

1. Heat olive oil in a skillet on high heat. When the oil shimmers, add the tenderloin and sear for 2 minutes on each side, turning it over four times to turn golden brown (8-10 minutes total). Add the cream and lower the heat to medium-low to maintain a simmer for 15-16 minutes to an internal temperature of 145°F (safe internal temperature), turning it over at 4-minute intervals.

2. In the meantime, prepare the pesto in a blender. Add the garlic, basil, cheese, pine nuts, and oil. Pulse to the desired consistency. If it's not right for you, you may need to add basil or oil to correct it.

3. After 10 minutes of simmering, add the pesto and continue to simmer to the pork tenderloin's proper internal temperature.

4. When 155°F internal temperature has been reached, remove from the heat, slice the tenderloin in thick fillets, plate with the cream sauce, and may be accompanied by roasted carrots, grilled asparagus, or rice and with pureed potatoes.

Pork Rib Steaks at the Modena Style. Inspired by (Wesevich, 2014)

This recipe reverses the browning and subsequent Maillard reactions, doing them at the end after the braising.

Ingredients for six servings:

- Protein   Pork rib steaks six.

- Fat   Unsalted butter 1 ½ Tbsp

- Aromatics   Rosemary leaves fresh 1 tsp

     Garlic 4 cloves pressed.

     Balsamic vinegar 1 Tbsp

- Seasoning   Kosher salt and freshly ground

     pepper to taste.

- Simmering liquid White wine dry ½ cup.

Beef broth 1 ½ cup.

Procedure:

1. Mix the aromatics and the seasoning to form a paste, then apply it to both sides of the pork chops.

2. Add a light layer of cooking olive oil After heating a heavy skillet large enough to fit the chops. Place the chops in the skillet, add the broth, which should cover the ribs, cover the skillet partially, and let the broth simmer. When the ribs begin to fry, sear both sides to golden brown.

3. Then add the wine and allow it to evaporate as well. Check the internal temperature of the pork chops; if 160°F, they are ready to serve, accompanied by vegetables of your choice.

Pork Steak a la Modena with carrots puree and mirepoix

Pork Chops in Plum Sauce. Inspired by (Mandy)

Ingredients for four servings:

- Protein   Pork chops 4.

- Carbohydrates   Corn starch 1 Tbsp

                             Plum puree 1 cup

- Fat   Canola oil one tab spoon

                             Cooking spray, 3 seconds' spray.

- Seasoning   Kosher salt and freshly ground black pepper.

- Flavorings   Lemon zest 1 tsp

                             Cinnamon, ground, ½ tsp

                             Cloves ground ¼ tsp

- Liquid   Red, sweet wine Like Marsala or sweet sherry ½ cup, Port will work too...

Procedure:

1. Remove some of the excess fat from the chops. Season them with salt and pepper on both sides and dust them with flour. Preheat the oven to 325 degrees F.

2. Heat a heavy, large skillet. When hot, add oil and cooking spray, and place the chops in it. When golden

brown (about 2 minutes per side) on both sides, put them on a cooking sheet and rest.

3. Mix the plum puree with the lemon zest, cinnamon, cloves, and wine. Pour over the chops and roast them at 325°F for about 40- 60 minutes. Check the internal temperature when it reaches 160°F; they are done.

4. Serve with vegetables of your choice; remember to decide whether you want to reinforce the sweetness or counter it.

Pork Chops Tuscany Style. *Inspired by **(Matherne, 2021)***

Ingredients for six servings:

- Protein   Pork chops 6

- Fat   Unsalted butter 1 Tbsp

  ½ cup of olive oil

- Aromatics   Garlic 3 cloves

  Fennel seeds 1 tsp

  Roma tomatoes four concasse.

- Seasoning   Kosher salt to taste.

- Produce   Baby spinach, 3 cups.

  Peaches, fresh peeled and cut in

  Eight slices, six fruits.

- Liquid   White wine dry, 1 cup.

Procedure:

1. Wash and dry the pork chops. Heat the skillet with oil and the garlic cloves at high heat, sear and brown the chops, and then retire the garlic cloves.

2. Add the wine and the fennel seeds, add the spinach, cover, and simmer at medium heat for 2-3 minutes for the spinach to wilt moderately. Remove the skillet from the fire, transfer the contents to a serving platter, and cover with an aluminum foil tent.

3. Melt the butter in another skillet, add the peach slices, and warm them up. Remove the skillet from the heat and serve the pork chops, sauce, and peaches.

4. It may be accompanied by glazed pearl onions with raisins and walnuts (recipe follows).

Glazed Pearl Onions with Raisins and Walnuts. Inspired by (Lopez-Alt J. K., 2018)

Ingredients for six servings:

- Star Ingredients   Pearl onions 2 lb.

  Raisins ½ cup.

- Fat   Unsalted butter 2 Tbsp

- Carbohydrates   Sugar 2 Tbsp or Stevia 2

  Tbsp

- Liquids   Water ¼ cup

  Sherry sweet 1 cup

  Balsamic vinegar   4 tsp

- Seasonings   Kosher salt and freshly ground black pepper, to taste.
- Flavorings   Thyme leaves, fresh, chopped 1 tsp Walnuts, cracked 2/3 cup.

Procedure:

Cook the onions:

1. Add the onions to a pot of salted boiling water and cook for 3-4 minutes. Drain the water and cool the onions slightly. Cut their root ends and squeeze the stem ends, and the onions will slip off their skins.

Simmer the onions.

2. Place the onions, sherry, raisins, water, and thyme in a large skillet. Bring to a boil, reduce the heat to a very low temperature, cover, and slow simmer until the onions begin to caramelize (45 minutes), stirring often.
3. Let the mixture cool some, then stir in the walnuts and balsamic vinegar. If it is too dry, add a few tsp of water.
4. Serve while still warm.

Braised Pork Belly Inspired by (Rolek, 2022)

Ingredients:

- Pork Brine, cold.   Lemons halved; five lemons. 12 bay leaves, parsley leaves one bunch, thyme sprigs one oz,

½ cup clover honey,

One head of garlic halved lengthwise,

¼ cup black peppercorns,

Two cups of kosher salt,

two gallons of water.

- Pork Belly   2 ½ lb. slab of pork belly, skin removed.

- Flavoring agents   Kosher salt and freshly ground black pepper.

2-3 cups of beef stock, warmed.

Procedure:

1. Brine the pork belly in the refrigerator for 2-hrs. (Brine has acid)

2. Remove the pork (discard the brine), rinse under cold water and dry or air dry.

3. Preheat oven to 325°F.

4. Season the pork belly with salt and pepper. Place it in an oven-proof sauté pan large enough to hold it comfortably.

5. Place the belly in the oven's top burner at medium-low heat and cook until it begins to render fat. Continue to cook until the fat is golden brown (15'). Pour the fat off as the belly cooks.

6. Remove the belly from the pan and pour the remaining fat. Return the belly to the pan, spoon enough stock to come ½ way up the pork belly, cover with parchment paper, and return to the oven for 2 ½ hours, checking every hour until tender.

7. Turn the belly over, baste with the pan juices, and return to the oven uncovered for 10 minutes to glaze the meat.

8. Remove from the oven, check internal temperature (safe temperature 145°F), let it cool, cover it with plastic wrap, press it with a weighted baking dish, and refrigerate for 12 hrs. We are keeping it covered with the basting liquid. It may be kept for up to 3 days. To serve, heat it in a 400°F oven with the fat layer down and enough braising liquid to cover ¼ of the meat thickness. Get to a simmer in the oven top and then to the oven for 15', turn the meat over, and return for 5' or so, basting every 2 minutes until richly browned and glazed.

9. Reduce the remaining braising liquid to a sauce consistency.

Braised Pork Shoulder. (Stewart, 2019) (Yanuq, n.d.)

Ingredients for eight servings:

- Protein   Bone in Pork shoulder, brought to room temperature.

- Carbohydrate   Corn starch 3 tbsp For thickening sauce.

- Fat   Pancetta or bacon, finely chopped.

Olive oil 2 Tbsp

- Aromatics   Red onion, medium-sized, sliced thin.

  Garlic, one head minced.

  Fennel seeds, toasted and ground.

  Coriander seeds, ground.

  Apples, granny cubed small 2

  Celeriac (celery root) peeled, cubed small.

  Corn, frozen 1 cup

  Lima Beans canned, one can.

- Seasoning   Kosher salt and freshly ground black pepper.

- Braising Liquid   Beer lager or cider 2 cups

  Chicken stock, low sodium, 1 cup.

Procedure:

Prep the ingredients:

Preheat the oven to 300°F (149°C)

1. sear and brown the pork shoulder on all sides in a Dutch oven or large pot. Then, put the shoulder in a rack.

2. Cook the pancetta or bacon to make it well done. Set it aside.

3. Prepare the sofrito or Matignon. Using the rendered fat from the pork shoulder and bacon, cook the onions; when translucent, add the celeriac and apples. When onions are nearly caramelized, add the seed flavorings and garlic.

Begin the simmer:

4. Add the braising liquid, bring to a simmer, cover the Dutch oven or pot, and place in the oven. Bake for 4 hours. The meat should fall off the bone.

5. Using two forks, shred the meat like it is for pulled pork. Serve with cooked vegetables (á la Matignon).

6. Using a fat separator or skimming, the remaining liquid separates the fat from the juices and thickens the juices with equal parts by volume corn starch and cold water. Add the slurry progressively, bringing the mixture to a boil until the addition does not thicken the sauce any longer, au jus consistency.

7. May be accompanied with cheesy grits or roasted potatoes.

Braised (Pulled) Pork with Matignon (succotash)

Pork Adobo Arequipa Style. *Inspired by (Yanuq, n.d.)*

Arequipa is a city in Perú, located southeast of Lima, on the skirts of the Andes, under a volcano named Misti (19,101 feet). Adobo is a noun from the verb adobe that means marinate or rub raw ingredients, like meats, fish, or vegetables. The term's origin is from Spain. Each of the old Spanish Colonies had a somewhat different version depending on the availability of some ingredients.

Ingredients for four servings:

- Protein   Pork tenderloin one lb. cut in

  large cubes.

- Aromatics   Rocoto paste 1 Tbsp

  Garlic 2 cloves large pressed.

Onions medium size, two sliced thick,

One is sliced lengthwise.

Oregano 2-3 sprigs or 1 tbsp of leaves.

Rue herb one sprig

Cumin ground 1 tsp

One habanero (Ají Limo) whole.

- Seasoning   Kosher salt to taste.

  Vinegar of wine, 2 Tbsp

- Simmering liquid   Chicha de Jora or light lager,

  enough to cover the meat.

Procedure:

1. Marinate the pork tenderloin pieces in Vinegar, chicha de Jora or beer, garlic, ajies (chilies) paste, and whole cumin, rue, the two onions sliced. Marinate overnight.

2. Place the marinade and meat in a large pot large enough to accommodate the ingredients comfortably. Cook at medium-high heat until the liquids become a sauce consistency. Cover the back of a soup spoon and leave a strip when wiping with a fingertip (nappe). About halfway, add the third onion, the one cut lengthwise.

3. The adobo is ready when the sauce thickens, and the meat is tender.

4. Serve with boiled potatoes or rice pilaf style.

Braising Beef

Cuts of Meat for Braising and Stewing.

Braising and stewing consist of cooking meats, fish, or vegetables by sautéing in fat and simmering in small amounts of liquid. The attributes of the meat should be a somewhat dense cut, with collagenous tissue in it, and enough fat to make the taste better. These attributes make these cuts unsuitable for grilling or only sautéing or frying. The long-simmering dissolves the tough collagenous tissues (membranes and tendons), and the rendered fat gives a tasteful flavor.

The cuts of meat with these characteristics may come from the forequarters or the hindquarters.

The cut from the forequarters most suitable for braising are Top blade steak, Shoulder braising steak, chuck eye steak, Mock filet steak, and beef shank.

The cuts from the hindquarter are mostly high-quality cuts such as porterhouse, T-bone, strip, sirloin, etc. The ones available for stewing are stewing steak, diced steak, stewing beef, and diced beef. They are cut off from trimming the better-quality cuts.

These stewing cuts are Stewing steaks, Diced steaks, Stewing Beef, and Diced Beef. An exemption is a shank steak from the hindquarter, an excellent braising cut.

Braised Short Ribs.
Inspired by (Garten, 2022) (Cellar Wine Club, 2021)

Ingredients for six servings:

- Protein   Short ribs, bone inn, cut across 5 lbs.

- Seasoning   Kosher salt and freshly ground black pepper to taste.

- Fast   Olive oil 3 Tbsp

- Carbohydrates   Flour all-purpose 3 Tbsp

- Aromatics   Onions white, medium size, cubed medium 3.

  Carrots, peeled, cubed medium.3

  Celery stalks, cubed medium 2.

  Tomato, paste 1 Tbsp

  Sprigs flat-leaf parsley 10.

  Sprigs of thyme 8.

  Oregano, sprigs 4.

  Rosemary sprigs 2.

  Bay leaves 2.

  Garlic 1 head, cut transversally.

  Cumin ground ½ tsp

- Simmering liquid   Red wine dry one bottle

  Beef stock was reduced by

  half 4 cups of the reduced.

Procedure:

Sear the short ribs.

1. Preheat oven to 350°F. Season the short ribs with salt and pepper. Heat a large Dutch oven; when hot, add oil; when shimmering, sear the short ribs on all sides by batches, about 8 minutes per batch. Transfer short ribs to a plate. Pour off all but 3 Tbsp of drippings from the pot.

Prepare the base (mirepoix).

2. Add onions, celery, and carrots to the pot and cook over medium heat, stirring often until the onions are browned (±5 minutes). Then add flour and tomato paste, stirring constantly until well combined and deep red (2-3 minutes). Stir in wine, and then add the short ribs and any juices. Bring to a boil, lower the heat to medium, and simmer until the wine is reduced by half (±25 minutes). Add the herbs and garlic, stir in the beef stock, boil, cover, and transfer to the oven.

3. Cook until the short ribs are tender (2-2 ½ hours). Transfer the short ribs to a platter. Strain the sauce and separate the fat with a fat separator, or skim it out and discard it. Season the sauce with salt and pepper. Serve in shallow bowls over mashed potatoes or rice. Spoon the sauce over. Alternatively, you may cool and refrigerate the whole thing overnight. The excess fat will be a congeal solid, so remove and discard it. Heat it in the stove or oven before serving.

A very similar dish is Beef Daube, where the meat used is beef chuck cut into cubes, and the base is prepared using bacon as a source of the fat to cook the onions and garlic. The meat is seared and browned in the bacon fat. The meat, onions, garlic, and bacon are in a large bowl. In the pot, a roux is made by adding flour to the fat; when the roux turns brown, add the reserved marinade, bring it to a boil, and scrape the bottom to recover the fat. Then, add the meat, bacon, garlic, and onion mixture. Simmer covered until meat is tender (about 2 hours). Uncover and continue to simmer until the meat is very tender and the liquid has reduced to the consistency of a sauce ($\pm$ 45 minutes). Remove the onions, carrots, bay leaves, and herb sprigs. Serve as the previous recipe.

Ground Beef Stew. Inspired by (Rattray, 2023)
Ingredients for four servings:

- Protein   Ground beef 85/15 1 lb.

- Carbohydrates   Flour 4 Tbsp

- Aromatics   Onion, medium size, red, cubed medium.

  Garlic 2 cloves, large.

  Carrots, peeled, medium size, thinly sliced 2.

  Tomatoes, diced one can of 14.5 oz

- Simmering Liquid   Beef stock, low sodium reduced to 3 cups.

	Water ¼ cup, cold for slurry for thickening sauce.
• Seasonings	Kosher salt and freshly ground black pepper to taste.
• Produce	Frozen mixed vegetables. Potatoes, peeled, diced 2 lbs.
• Garnish	Parsley, chopped 2 Tbsp

Procedure:

1. Heat a large Dutch oven or a deep, heavy skillet on medium-high heat. Add the ground beef; as it releases some fat, add the onions and cook until translucent. Stir frequently. When the meat has browned, drain the excess fat. Return to the heat, add the Beef stock, carrots, and potatoes, cover the pan, reduce the heat to low, and cook for 20 minutes. At the 10-minute mark, add the diced tomatoes.

2. In the meantime, prepare the flour slurry by mixing 4 Tbsp of flour with ¼ cup of cold water and dissolve it completely.

3. When the stew is ready and the meat is fully cooked, add the frozen mixed vegetables and cook for a minute or two. Gradually add the flour slurry, bring the stew to a boil, and continue to add the slurry, stirring, until it no longer thickens the sauce.

4. Serve over rice pilaf style or over couscous.

Braising Lamb

Lamb in Cilantro, Cumin, and Chili Sauce. (Seco de Cordero) (Chard, 2013)

Ingredients for eight servings:

- Protein size

  Lamb shoulder one lb. diced in bite

  pieces.

- Carbohydrates

  White potatoes, small ½ lb. Peeled

  and it halved also.

- Fat

  Olive oil light. 2 Tbsp

- Aromatics small.

  Carrots, large, peeled one, cubed

  Onion, medium size, peeled and

  cubed large.

  Garlic 3 cloves, large.

  Ají Amarillo paste 2 tsp

  Jalapeño, seedless, cubed finely,

  one.

  Cilantro ½ cup, blended with olive

  oil into a paste.

  Cumin ground, 1 tsp

- Produce

  Peas, frozen ½ cup.

- Seasoning   Kosher salt and freshly ground black pepper to taste.

- Simmering liquid Lamb stock enough to cover the meat (cubes or veal demiglace).

Procedure:

1. Season the meat with salt, pepper, and cumin. Heat a large saucepan or a deep skillet. When hot, add the oil. When the oil shimmers, add the seasoned meat, sear and brown it, then remove it and set aside.

2. In the same pan, sauté the onions, garlic, carrots, and jalapeño. When the onions are translucent, add the lamb meat and stir to coat it with the pan juices.

3. Add the cilantro paste and stir it. Add the lamb stock, just enough to cover the meat. Cover the pan, reduce the heat to low, and simmer for 20 minutes.

4. At this point, add the potatoes on top; do not mix. Put the cover back on and simmer for another 15 minutes. The potatoes and meat should be tender and cooked through.

5. You may add rinsed canned Cannellini beans to warm them. Serve rice and stew over it, including the cannellini and vegetables.

Lamb Chops in Seco Sauce Inspired by
(Chard,   /recipes/margots-seco-de-cordero-peruvian-lamb-stew/, 2013)

This dish is like the previous one; instead of a stew, it is more of a braise. The sauce is essentially the same; the chops are sauté until nearly done, then finished for a few minutes in the sauce.

Ingredients for two servings:

- Marinade   Chicken broth ½ cup.

  ¼ + ¼ cup of olive oil.

  Garlic minced 2 + 1 Tbsp

  ¼ tsp of ground cumin.

  Salt and pepper to taste.

  Chopped flat-leaf parsley 2 Tbsp

- Protein   Lamb chops 4.

- Aromatics   Onions, red, cubed medium ¼ cup.

  Jalapeño paste 1 Tbsp (blend

  jalapeño in a little olive oil).

  Cumin, ground, ¼ tsp

  Cilantro leaves 2 cups.

- Carbohydrates   Rice, cooked pilaf style 1 cup.

- Braising liquid   Beef or lamb stock 1 cup.

Procedure:

1. Combine all the marinating ingredients except the additional olive oil and garlic in a large bowl. Add the chops and refrigerate for at least 2 hours.

2. When cooking, heat the remaining oil over medium-low and add the onions, garlic, and cumin. Stir occasionally until the onions are soft and barely past the translucent state (8-10 minutes).

3. In the meantime, add the cilantro paste with water to the onion mixture; if necessary, add one or two tbsp of water. Sauté the chops in a different skillet, flipping them but not overcooking them. Transfer them to the sauce and cook them for a few minutes to an internal temperature of 125°F for medium rare. When you serve them over rice, the temperature will be 130°F, a safe temperature for lamb. If the sauce is too thin, use corn starch slurry, equal parts starch and water by volume.

4. Serve them over rice pilaf style, with the sauce over both.

Braised Lambchops in Seco sauce

Braised Lamb Shanks. Inspired by (Benites, Pierna de Cordero)

226

Ingredients for 4-6 servings:

- Protein   Lamb Shanks trimmed of excess fat. 4-6.
- Fat   Olive Oil 2 Tbsp
- Carbohydrates   Flour ¼ cup.
- Aromatics   Onion, white, large, diced medium 1.
  Garlic, minced, six cloves large.
  Carrots, sliced 1/2 -inch thick, 2.
  Tomato, canned, puree 14 oz
  Tomato paste, 2 Tbsp
  Rosemary leaves, chopped, 2 Tbsp
  Parsley or cilantro, fresh, finely chopped, 2 Tbsp
  Bay leaves 2
- Flavoring   Beef bouillon cubes two or beef base better than bouillon 1 tsp
- Simmering liquid   Wine, red, dry, 1 ½ cup.
  Beef stock reduced to half, 2 cups.
  White wine vinegar 1 Tbsp
- Seasoning   Kosher salt and freshly ground pepper to taste.

Procedure:

1. Preheat oven to 350 degrees Fahrenheit.

2. Heat oil in a Large Dutch oven. Wash the lamb shanks and dry them with paper towels.

3. When oil shimmers, sear two shanks until golden brown. Repeat with the remaining shanks. Transfer to a plate and reserve.

4. In the same pot, add the onions and carrots, sauté until softened (± 3 minutes), then add garlic and cook for 1 minute—season with salt and pepper.

5. Add the flour, sprinkle it, mix well, and cook to brown and thicken the sauce. Add the stock, wine, pureed tomato, tomato paste, beef bouillon or beef base, and herbs. Add the shanks, stir, cover, and bring to the oven.

6. Simmer for 2 ½ hours. The meat should be super tender and fall away from the bone. Adjust the heat so it simmers at a slow rate.

7. Carefully transfer the shanks to a plate so they do not fall apart. Cover with tented foil.

8. Continue to cook the sauce on the stove to thicken it; if it is too thin, add a slurry of cornstarch. Skim any excess fat from the surface.

9. Garnish with parsley leaves and serve with mashed potatoes, rice, or pasta. You may let it cool and refrigerate it to serve the next day. Place the pot on the stove over medium-low heat for 15 minutes at a gentle simmer, then serve.

Non-Conventional Meats

Tripe

Mondongo a la Italiana (Tripe Italian Style). (Acurio, Comidas Peruanas, 2023)

This Peruvian dish originated from the Italian Immigrants in Perú during the mid- to late 1800s. Other Italian dishes include Hunter's chicken stew. ***Hunter Chicken Stew (Pollo alla Cacciatore)***.

Inspired by , and Veal Marsala *Veal Marsala*.

Ingredients for six servings:

- Protein   Precooked Tripe 1 lb. cut in strips of 3 by ½ inches.

- Carbohydrates   Potatoes cut as for French fries 1 ½ lb. I like to parboil before frying them.

- Aromatics   Onion, red, large, one cubed medium.

  Tomato, plump, large, one cubed.

  Garlic 3-4 cloves pressed.

  Ají Panca paste 4 Tbsp

  Tomato, paste 4 tsp

  Bay leaf 2

- Produce   Mushrooms Shitake. 4 oz halved.

  Green peas ¼ cup.

Carrots are cut into sticks, one large.

- Seasoning   Kosher salt and freshly ground black pepper.

  Cumin ground 1 tsp

- Simmering Liquid White wine dry 2 Tbsp to recover the fond.

  One cup of the broth from boiling the tripe.

Procedure:

1. In a stock pot with 5 quarts of hot water, add salt and flavorings for the water, such as garlic, ginger, and habanero pepper. Cut in half; avoid leafy herbs so as not to stain the tripe. Boil the solution and then add the tripe for 40-45 minutes. The tripe should be tender when pricked with a fork.

2. Remove the tripe and allow it to cool enough to handle. Cut it into stripes about three by ½ inches. Save a cup of broth.

3. Heat a heavy, large skillet or Dutch oven on medium heat. When hot, add oil and heat to the shimmer state. Then, stir the aromatics, particularly the garlic, to avoid burning them. Cook for a few minutes, adding the seasoning to your taste.

4. Add the white wine and scrape the bottom of the pan to integrate the fond. Add the broth from cooking the tripe.

Then add the precooked tripe, carrots, green peas, and potatoes. Cook until the potatoes are soft but not falling apart.

5. When ready, serve with rice in pilaf style, sprinkle with cilantro and parmesan cheese.

Beef or Veal Tongue, Larded. Inspired by (Benites, Lengua Mechada)

Ingredients for six servings:

- Protein   Beef tongue one.

- Fat   Olive oil ½ cup.

                 Bacon 5 oz

- Aromatics   Thyme, oregano, cilantro, two sprigs of each bundled and tied together.

                 Garlic cloves, large, 4 pressed.

                 Black peppercorn whole 10

                 Onion powder 2 Tbsp and one medium

                 size cubed small.

                 Clove one spike.

                 Bay leaf 2

                 Pimenton (smoked paprika) 2 tsp

                 Tomato puree 1 cup.

- Seasonings   Kosher salt and freshly ground black

pepper to taste.

- Liquid   White wine dry four fluid oz

                                     Beef broth reduced by half to 1 quart.

Procedure:

1. Clean the tongue, scraping the skin all over with the spine of a knife (opposite to the edge). Wash it in running cold water. Boil it in salt water, the herbs bundle, bay leaves, and peppercorns. Boil it until it begins to soften. Remove the pot from the heat and set it aside to cool some of the liquid used for boiling. Once it is cool enough to handle, remove the skin. Rub the meat with salt, ground pepper, onion powder, and pimentón. Lard the tongue with segments of bacon, about half of the bacon.

2. Sauté the tongue in olive oil, then add the remaining aromatics (cubed onion), the cloves, tomato puree, and bacon in small pieces.

3. Cook at medium heat; add the beef broth in aliquots (small amounts) to avoid things drying up; regulate the heat down if it is boiling too much; want to keep it at a simmer. When the meat is tender, it is done. Test it with a fork. Mild resistance is okay, but no higher.

4. Serve in slices with the sauce, accompanied by roasted potatoes and rice pilaf.

Veal Kidneys in Sherry Sauce. Inspired by (Benites, Riñones al Jerez)

Ingredients for six servings:

- Protein   6 veal kidneys
- Carbohydrates   Flour, all-purpose, toasted 1 Tbsp
- Fat   ½ cup olive oil light.
- Aromatics   Onion, red ½ lb. cubed medium.

                 Garlic, cloves large, 3 pressed.

                 Bay leaf 1

- Seasoning   Kosher salt and freshly ground

                 black pepper to taste.

- Simmering liquid   Juice of 6 limes.

                 Beef broth reduced by half to 1 quart.

                 Sherry amontillado ½ cup

Procedure:

1. Clean the fat around the kidneys. Slice them in half lengthwise. Remove the ducts from the center of the inward periphery. Wash them with lime juice and drain them in a colander.

2. Dry rub them with salt, pepper, and garlic pulp. Pour half the oil over them in a zip-lock plastic bag, add the bay leaf, and marinate for 2-3 hours.

3. At the proper time, heat a heavy large skillet on medium heat; add the remaining olive oil. When shimmering, add half of the onion. When translucent, cut the kidneys into bite-size pieces and the marinating mixture. Cover and simmer, adding the broth to avoid drying the stew. Add the remaining half of the onion and the toasted flour,

stirring well. Add the sherry, cook for a minute, and serve immediately. It may be accompanied by rice pilaf style or roasted potatoes.

Rabbit Stew. Inspired by (Benites, Estofado de Conejo)

Ingredients for six servings:

- Protein   Rabbit of about 3 lbs.
- Carbohydrate   Potatoes, small 1 ½ lbs.
- Fat   Olive oil light, 1 cup.
- Seasoning   Kosher salt 2 Tbsp
- Aromatics   Garlic 2 cloves, pressed.

  Onion's red, medium size, cubed medium 2.

  Oregano dry 1 tsp

  Tomato concasse 2.
- Acid   Vinegar or lime juice 2 Tbsp
- Simmering liquid   Sherry ¼ cup.

Procedure:

1. Wash the rabbit in water with vinegar or lime juice. Cut the portions. Mix the salt, garlic, onions, oregano, and tomatoes in a bowl. Rub the mix on the rabbit pieces.

2. Heat the oil in a Dutch oven or deep skillet until shimmering. Add the rabbit pieces and the rub's seasonings. Cook at low heat for 20 minutes. Add ¼ cups of hot water or Sherry and cook at low heat for 60 more minutes. At the 45-minute mark, add the potatoes.

3. When done, the meat should be tender, and the potatoes should show little resistance to being picked with a paring knife tip.

4. Serve with the sauce and potatoes.

Plank Cooking.

This method originated in the Pacific Northwest among Native American tribes and was copied by colonizers. Wild food meats, fish, and poultry mostly taste better when cooked in planks; it is an easy cooking technique, and the food looks great. Good information can be obtained from Cooking with Cedar Planks 101 (Wild Alaskan Company, 2021) and a Beginner's Guide to Cedar Plank Grilling (Nicole Doster, 2020). Notice that Plank Cooking can be done on the Grill or the Oven.

When cooking in planks, you should be aware of a few things:

- Only use food-safe untreated planks; Cedar, alder, and hickory are most used.

- Check for splinters.

- Presoak, totally submerged, for 1-2 hours for grilling. You may use shorter times if cooking in an oven.

- When grilling, be aware of possible flare-ups; it is best to use 2-zone grilling.

- Pre-charring the planks increases the flavor.

- Oil the fish and food side of the plank.

- Flavorings (herbs, spices, etc.) work well.

- Cook to the internal temperatures of the food product.

- In addition to fish, scallops, lobster, shrimp, chicken, pork, vegetables, and beef can be cooked in planks.

- Reusing planks will depend on the degree of char present, general damage, and care given. Wash them with water, soak them, and freeze them for subsequent use.

Wild Salmon on a Plank.

1. Soak your plank in water, especially on first use. The natural flavors will be at their best then.

2. Prepare the salmon, leaving the skin on. Check for stray scales and remove them.

3. If you are cooking an entire filet, fold over the thin portions to obtain a uniform thickness and secure them with toothpicks.

4. Place a pan covered with tin foil or parchment paper under the rack where the plank will be to catch any juices that may fall off.

5. Oil the fish and the plank surface where the fish will be. Season the fish with salt and pepper and add any flavorings you wish.

6. Preheat the oven to 350°F and bake to the fish's internal temperature. When it reaches 125°F, it is medium rare. You can also check by flaking the thickest part of the fish to see if all the translucent areas are cooked now.

CHAPTER 12

This chapter will review methods of preserving and flavoring food without heat, such as Curing, fermenting, pickling, and souring.

Since the appearance of the species of homo sapiens and the discovery of fire, food has been preserved and flavored by the utilization of heat. They had to be surrounded by fruits, vegetables, seafood, birds, and other animals that became not so tasty after exposure to the hot sun, did not take long to smell foul, and probably induced illness.

Therefore, the preservation of food products may be the cause of developing techniques such as brining (salt or salty water), Marinating (using acid), and Pickling with salty solutions (allows for fermented pickles) or with acid (unfermented pickles). Some pickling techniques combine acid with sugar, such as when pickling products such as turnips, jicama, onions, etc.

Fermentation dates to 7000 BC in China. Good bacteria preserve and transform fermented food products. Usually, carbohydrates and sugar are converted into carbon dioxide, acids, and alcohols. These compounds preserve the food and add to its flavor. Fermentation promotes the growth of probiotics, so it has beneficial effects on the gastrointestinal tract.

Salmon was preserved for transport issues initially and for flavorings later.

Smoked salmon is first treated with immersion in a salt brine and later smoked. Depending on the temperature, it can be cold-smoked or hot-smoked.

Lox is salt-cured but not smoked.

Gravlax is salt-cured, following the Scandinavian tradition, with dill and sugar added. Some preparations may have other additions. It is not smoked.

Later, different preparations appeared, like ceviche's first appearance in the Inca culture, even before the limes and lemons were brought to the Americas by the colonizers. They use the acid of Passion Fruit (Maracuya), a fruit from the Amazon Basin, and later the juice of lime. The amount of time the food product is in the acid solution varies; most specialized restaurants will serve them within minutes of the preparation. Other establishments may keep them refrigerated for a more extended period. Sashimi has a long history, too, and originated in Asia (Japan). Later, Crudo appeared in restaurant menus, and this is a more generic term for uncooked seafood.

Pickling Vegetables

- Vegetables of choice: Sliced, then any of the following or a mix: Jicama, Purple turnip, Daikon, pearl onions, or slices of red onions, cucumbers, or radishes.

- Flavoring: mustard seeds, Thyme, garlic peeled and bruised, and cloves.

- Marinating solution: 2 cups of water, 1 cup of white wine vinegar, 200 g of sugar or stevia granulated about the same amount.

Procedure:

- Prep your vegetables and place them in an empty pickling bottle, the bottle boiled. Fill the bottle without packing it.

- Mix the pickling solution with the sugar, heat it, and add the sugar, stirring. When all is mixed, and the solution is still warm, fill the bottle containing the vegetables, let it cool some more, and then refrigerate.

- May be consumed one week later.

Pickled Turnips, Chinese Style (Wang, 1973)

Ingredients for six servings:

- 2 lbs. of turnips or daikon, cut into thin slices.

- Rice vinegar 1 cup.

- 1/3 cup of sugar

- ½ Tbsp of salt, refined into tiny grains.

- two habaneros or jalapeños, seedless, cut in fine strips.

- Black pepper ground coarse.

Procedure:

1. Cut the turnips into thin circumferential slices.

2. Lay them flat on a large platter, as much as possible, in a single layer. Dust them with the refined salt and rest them with the salt for ½ hours.

3. Wash them in cold tap water, squeezing them to remove the gummy stuff the salt pools in. Repeat this as much as necessary to keep the slices crisp and not sticky. Then, dry them on paper towels and put them back in a large bowl.

4. Place them in a canning bottle, alternating turnip, ají, and pepper layers.

5. Meanwhile, heat the marinade to a boil. Turn the heat off and let it cool to 175°F.

6. Then, pour the marinating solution into the bottle. It should contain vinegar, sugar, and salt. Refrigerate and let the turnips and chilis pickle for two weeks before consuming them.

Note: You may use radishes instead of turnips; better yet, you can use Daikon (Chinese winter turnip).

Pickled Daikon

Recipes of No-heat Cooked Meats

Cured Striped Bass

This dish cures the fish with a distilled, high alcohol content spirit, Grappa or Pisco. Grappa is an Italian Spirit made with grape residue after making wine. Pisco is a Peruvian spirit made from grapes specifically grown to produce Pisco. No wine is made from these grapes.

Ingredients for one fillet:

Protein	One two lb. filet of Striped Bass, with skin, scaled.
Aromatics	Onion red, finely sliced Tamed with salt and hot water.
	Fennel seeds toasted 1 Tbsp
	Fennel fronds of one bulb
Seasonings	Kosher Salt ¼ cup.
	Sugar 2 Tbsp
Grappa or Pisco	1 cup.

Procedure:

1. On a glass baking container, spread the onions (after taming) in the shape of the filet, and top the onions with most of the fronds of the fennel. Save some for garnish)

2. mix the sugar, fennel seeds, and salt in a small bowl and sprinkle the mixture over the fennel fronds.

3. Place the fish, skin side up, over the curing mix, cover with plastic wrap, and set an appropriate-sized cooking

sheet over the filet—weigh down with heavy cans for 24 to 36 hours in the refrigerator.

4. To serve, scrape the remaining cure material, set the filet on a cutting board, slice thin fish slices diagonally, and leave behind the dark meat attached to the skin along the midline.

5. Serve fish slices over baguette toast, drizzled with olive oil and sprinkled lightly with kosher salt.

Crudo recipes.

The process of making or serving will be the same for all the following example recipes. In a Ramequin mix, add light olive oil (so the oil's flavor will not obscure the seafood's taste), kosher salt, lemon juice, a little Ají Amarillo paste, and a few chopped cilantro leaves. Mix them well just before applying them to the seafood. I would use 1-1 ½ tsp per serving.

Sea Scallop Crudo

Ingredients for two servings:

1. Sea scallops 2-3 thinly sliced circumferentially, arranged in the center of the plate.

2. Spoon small amounts of the oil, lemon juice, and salt over the slices of seafood.

3. Sprinkle a little of Maldon Sea salt flakes over.

4. Serve with toasted thin baguette toast.

Procedure:

1. Arrange sea scallops in the center of a plate.

2. Spoon small amounts of the oil, lemon juice, and salt over the slices of seafood.

3. Sprinkle a little of Maldon Sea salt flakes over.

4. Serve with toasted thin baguette toast.

Note: Instead of sea scallops, you may use thin slices of tuna belly, Arctic chard, king salmon, or other salmon, Corvina, or red snapper.

Recipes for Soured Meats.

Ceviche and Tiraditos

It is said that cooking requires subjecting the nutrients to a temperature of 120°C. However, boiling and poaching use lower temperatures and are considered cooking methods. The most likely thing to happen is that the product of temperature and time is a factor, explaining that cooking occurs at lower temperatures. The same can be said about the Sous vide cooking method, where relatively lower temperatures achieve complete cooking.

Preparing ceviche, tiraditos, and crudos uses no heat but depends on using acid from lime or lemon juices. This acid denatures the proteins, changing the texture and color of at least their surface. It is necessary to avoid fish that carry parasites or bacteria unless they have been flash-frozen to very low temperatures for 24 hours. The average home freezer doesn't achieve low enough temperatures, and the period of freezing needs to be at least a week. By then, the texture of the fish had changed primarily due to intracellular crystal formation that punctured the cell membranes. On thawing, the intracellular fluid mixes with the interstitial fluid (fluid between the cells). Both have very different chemical compositions; therefore, the taste also changes. Only the freshest fish will do for these dishes.

Recipes for Ceviche and Tiraditos.

Peruvian Ceviche

Ceviche of Porgy

INGREDIENTS

For the Leche de Tigre (ceviche sauce)

- 2/3 cup fresh lime juice

- two garlic cloves, smashed.

- one tablespoon (packed) chopped fresh cilantro leaves.

- 1/2 ají limo or habanero chili, seeded, halved lengthwise, or 2 tbsp ají amarillo sauce.

- 1/2 small red onion, chopped.

- 1/2 cup bottled clam juice (optional)

- Kosher salt

For the Ceviche

- Flounder or corvina, porgy, Black seabass 1 lb.

- One small red onion sliced thin and tamed.

- Kosher salt

- Cilantro leaves chopped 1 Tbsp

Procedure:

Leche de Tigre

1. Set a fine-mesh sieve over a small bowl. Purée the first four ingredients of the sauce and four large ice cubes in a blender and blend until smooth. Add 1/3 of the onions and pulse three times short. Stir clam juice if desired. Season with salt. Cover and chill.

Ceviche

2. Rub a large bowl with the other half of the split chili or add the ají amarillo paste. Add the fish, the other 2/3 of the sliced onions, and the leche de Tigre (ceviche sauce), stir well, and let marinate for 5-10 minutes—season with salt.

3. Tamed onions (see note) are used above.

4. Serve soon so the fish can cook quickly.

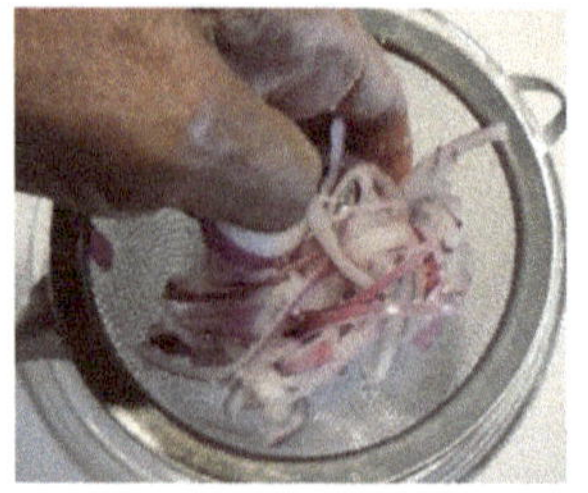
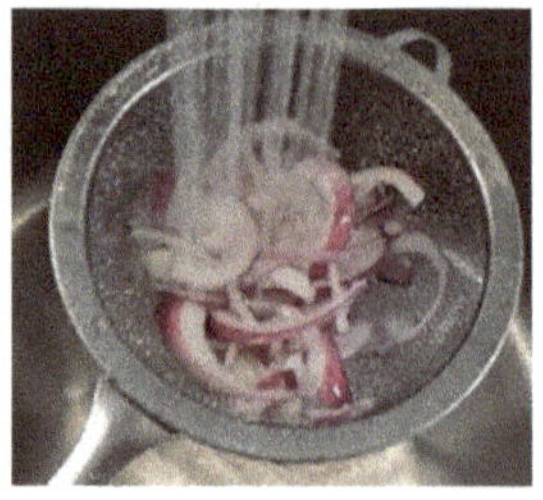

Cover with kosher salt   *Rub them with your*   *Rinse them with hot tap*

Note: I like to tame the raw onions by placing them in a colander, covering them with kosher salt, massaging them with your hand for a couple of minutes, and then rinsing them with hot water from the faucet. Allow them to dry for a few minutes, then proceed as above.

Tiradito of Corvina

Tiradito de corvina

Ingredients for two servings

- Protein   Corvina 200g. Alternatively, it could be flounder, porgy, or another white

- Aromatics

  8 Ají Amarillo without seeds or

  veins for the sauce, or ají amarillo paste.

  MSG 1 pinch

  Ají Limo to taste, cut thickly, can be removed before serving if desired.

- Acid

  Limes Juice of 5 fruits.

- Flavorings

  Cilantro leaves chopped 1 Tbsp

  Soy sauce 1 Tbsp

- Fat

  Olive oil 1 Tbsp to allow

  emulsification when blended.

- Ice

  2 Ice cubes to keep the preparation cold.

Procedure:

1. A serving is about 200 g and should be cut in a slant, not too thin or thick. Do not stretch the pieces (by banging them flat with the knife). The texture of the fish will be lost. You may need to wet the knife so the fish will not stick to it.

2. Place the fish on a chilled plate and prepare the sauce.

3. In a bowl, place a bit of unused fish, add 1 ½ Tbsp of ají amarillo paste, two ice cubes, and the lime juice. Soak

the ají habanero in the sauce for a few minutes and remove.

4. Remove the ice and blend it in a blender or food processor; it will form an emulsion.

5. Serve by placing the sauce over the well-placed fish. Decorate with cilantro and serve immediately.

Jicama, Mango, Zucchini Ceviche

This is not a classic ceviche, but it works well, particularly if combined with a firm white fish like corvina or black sea bass.

Ingredients for 4-6 servings:

- Corvina 1 lb. cut in 2 cm. cubes

- Jicama peeled and sliced thin in a mandolin.

- Mango peeled, cut in slices about 4-5 mm thick ¾ of a cup.

- The zucchini is peeled, cut in half lengthwise, all seeds removed, and cut in u-shaped slices 4 mm thick. ½ cup.

- Onion red, small, thinly sliced.

- Roma tomato, cubed, one.

- Seasoning kosher salt and freshly ground black pepper to taste.

- Lime juice of 6 limes.

- Orange juice ½ cup.

- Ponzu sauce 1 Tbsp

- Flavorings cilantro leaves, chopped ¼ cup. Ají amarillo paste ½ - 1 tsp

Procedure:

1. Mix the fish, jicama, mango, zucchini, onion, and tomato in a large bowl. Once uniformly mixed, add the liquids (ponzu, lime juice, and orange juice, and mix again to cover everything with the marinade. Add ají amarillo, salt, and pepper to taste.

2. Add a piece of boiled sweet potato and a segment of corn on the cob and toast.

Mushiame o Muchame

It is a preparation brought in by the men working the Italian ships in the eighteen hundreds. Traditionally, it was prepared with tenderloin of dolphin or sea lion. Later, because of regulations for protecting those species, it was changed to tenderloin of shark, swordfish, tuna, bonito, albacore, octopus, and beef. It is first cured with salt or a salty brine and then dried in a covered space (protected from rain) for 2-3 weeks, hanging until it has the consistency of a cold cut. Shake it to dispose of the excess salt and preserve it by freezing or submerging it in oil like a confit.

To serve, slice it thin, serve over toasted bread, water crackers, or soda crackers, with sauces like chimichurri, gremolata, thin slices of avocado or guacamole, thin slices of tomato, and may finish them with a bit of olive oil.

Octopus Mushiame (Muchame)

Ingredients for two servings:

- Protein   Octopus tentacles 8 oz

- Fat   ½ cup of olive oil

                   ½ avocado

- Aromatics   Tomato concasse one tomato,

                   cut into small cubes.

- Seasoning   Pepper to taste. No salt is needed.

Procedure:

Prepare the Brine.

1. Mix 2 cups of water.

2. 2 Tbsp of salt.

3. 1 Tbsp of sugar or stevia granulated.

4. Place the octopus tentacles in the brine, place them in the refrigerator, and let them brine for 24 hours or more.

5. Remove the octopus, dry it with paper towels, arrange it in a single layer on a platter, and allow it to dry for four hrs. in a warm and dry place.

6. Place the octopus in olive oil and submerge until ready to use.

7. Serve with the sauce.

Serving sauce #1:

Ingredients:

- Garlic 2 cloves diced small.

- ½ Tbsp oregano leaves chopped

- ½ Tbsp parsley chopped

- 100 ml. of olive oil

Process in a food processor. Sprinkle over the protein (octopus or other) on a platter, leaving no space between the protein slices.

We are serving sauce #2: Ginger, Miso, and cilantro sauce.

Ingredients:

- 1 ½ tsp roasted sesame oil

- ½ cup minced shallots

- Minced, peeled ginger 1 Tbsp

- 1 cup low-sodium chicken broth.

- ¼ cup of frozen orange concentrate thawed.

- Rice vinegar 3 Tbsp

- Yellow miso 2 Tbsp

- Cilantro leaves chopped 2 Tbsp

Procedure:

1. Heat a heavy small skillet, add sesame seed oil, and heat it until it shimmers.

2. Add shallots, ginger, and sauté for a few minutes.

3. Add broth, orange concentrate, and vinegar. Boil until it is reduced to ¾ cup (by half).

4. May prepare to this point one day ahead and chill it in a refrigerator.

5. Return to a boil, stir in miso and cilantro, simmer for a minute, and season with salt and pepper to taste.

Other Preparations

Tuna on Quinoa with two sauces. (Piquant Mayonnaise Sauce or Miso Shallots Orange Sauce).

This dish is hard to categorize. It certainly is not Sashimi, where the chef's management of the fish is essential; it is not ceviche or tiradito since the fish is not cured in lime or lemon juice. Is it crudo? But most crudos do not have a wholly accompanying ingredient. You be the judge and assign a category.

Ingredients for two servings:

- Tuna tender loin1 lb. sashimi quality; if you wish to sear the tuna, cut it into ½ inch cubes or thin slices. (Keep refrigerated until plating)

- Quinoa, mixed varieties 1 cup. Boiled with 1 ½ cups of dashi or water.

For sauce, 1 Miso, shallots, and orange sauce.

- 1 tsp oriental sesame oil

- ¼ cup minced shallots
- ½ Tbsp of grated, peeled ginger.
- ½ cup of Dashi.
- 2 Tbsp of frozen orange juice concentrated, thawed.
- 1 ½ Tbsp rice vinegar.
- 1 Tbsp Of yellow miso.
- 2 Tbsp of chopped cilantro leaves.

Preparation:

1. Heat oil in a small, heavy saucepan over medium heat. Add shallots and ginger and sauté for a couple of minutes.

2. Add Dashi, orange juice concentrate and vinegar. Reduce by boiling by 1/2, about 6 minutes.

3. Stir in miso stirring to obtain a smooth, thickened sauce. Add cilantro and mix.

4. Season with salt and pepper. It probably won't need much added salt.

For sauce 2:

- 1 Tbsp of mayonnaise.
- 1 tsp of ají amarillo paste.

Mix them thoroughly.

Procedure:

1. Apply either sauce around the quinoa set at the center of the plate (using a round or rectangular mold) or use a decorating bag to surround the quinoa with the sauce.

2. Place the tuna on top of the quinoa and squeeze a dollop of sauce in the center of the tuna.

Another good combination is a base of avocado salad, tuna seared as a second layer, and seaweed salad topped with it all. The combination of the different flavors and textures makes it a delicious dish.

Tuna Tower with avocado salad and seaweed salad layers

Salmon Mousse

This is another dish that requires more work to categorize. It uses smoked salmon that is cured and then smoked; all other ingredients are not heat-cooked.

Ingredients for 2 ½ cups:

- four oz cream cheese

- 4 oz of sour cream

- four oz smoked salmon

- 1 Tbsp of lemon juice

- 1 tsp of lemon zest

- Ají Amarillo paste 1 tsp

Procedure:

1. Place all ingredients in a food processor and blend until smooth.

2. Serve with dill, cappers, and chives on the side.

3. Serve with water crackers, small bread toast, or cucumber slices.

CHAPTER 13

Two methods have regional origins but have become universally practiced: fondues and Souffles. These two methods produce delightful dishes, so it is worthwhile learning them.

Fondue

Wikipedia defines Fondue (en.wikepedia org., 2024) as a Swiss national dish consisting of melted cheese in wine, served in a communal pot over a portable stove, heated with a candle or spirit lamp, and eaten with dipping bread or some other ingredient in the melted cheese.

Fondue has become so popular that there are Restaurants dedicated exclusively to this dish. The utensils used in the preparation and the ingredients are readily available.

There are variations; in some cases, cheese is not used, but other liquids may be, such as fondue bourguignon or seafood fondues, where a soup could be served from the simmering liquid at the end.

Fondue recipes have been developed that mimic the flavors of traditional dishes and are served in communal settings from a shared fondue pot. Ilana Simon, in her book The Fondue Bible (Simon, 1963), presents what she calls the 200 best recipes, including dishes like Fondue á la Coquilles St. Jacques, Paella

Fondue, Fondue a la Veal Parmesan, and dessert fondue like Caramel fondue.

Swiss Cheese Fondue Inspired by (Simon, 1963) Page 28.
Ingredients for 4-6 servings:

- Garlic 1 large clove halved across.

- 24 oz of grated Swiss cheeses (Gruyére, Emmentaler, raclette).

- White wine, dry 1 cup.

- 2 Tbsp cornstarch.

- Lemon juice 1 tsp

- Black pepper freshly ground one two-finger pinch.

- Freshly ground nutmeg, one three-finger pinch.

Dipping Ingredients:

Toasted country bread or pumpernickel cubes, steamed potatoes, pear or apple chunks, or assorted pickled or roasted vegetables.

Procedure:

1. Rub the inside of the fondue pot with garlic. Mix the cheese with the cornstarch. Prepare the dipping ingredients.

2. Heat the wine in the fondue pot, add the cheese progressively stirring, add the lemon juice, and cook at moderate heat until the cheese melts; reduce heat to low.

3. Serve immediately.

Notes:

- Often, mustard and spirits such as Kirsch, cognac, another spirit, or sherry are recommended to be added to the cheese fondue.

- The combination of cheeses can be modified as well; other cheeses recommended are Fontina and Gouda.

Blue Cheese Fondue Inspired by (Simon, 1963) Page 61.

Ingredients for four servings:

- Cream cheese 8oz cubed and at room temperature.

- Blue cheese crumbled, 4 oz

- Butter unsalted, 1 Tbsp

- Leeks white and light green parts only chopped ¼ cup.

- Red onion medium size ½ cubed small.

- Heavy cream 1/3 cup

- Milk whole 1/3 cup.

Procedure:

1. Mix blue cheese and cream cheese, mix well.

2. Melt butter in a large skillet. Add leeks and onion and cook over medium heat until soft. Stir in cream and milk and lower the heat to medium-low, avoiding boiling.

3. Add the cheese mixture progressively, whisking after each addition until melted. When done, transfer to a fondue pot, set to simmer, and serve immediately.

Fondue bourguignon

This is a variation of fondue that originated in New York at Konrad Egli's Restaurant Chalet Suisse in the 1950s. When perusing recipes for this dish by several celebrities, I found great latitude in Fondue bourguignon, from the closest, using beef broth and oil as the fondue liquid. It is prepared in the kitchen and served on a platter as the communal pot.

The closest to the classic Beef bourguignon is as follows.

Ingredients for six servings:

For the beef bouillon.

- Olive oil 1 Tbsp

- White onions, finely chopped 1 cup.

- Cloves garlic, pressed, two large.

- Beef broth, low sodium 5 cups.

- Red wine, dry ½ cup.

- Worcestershire sauce 1 Tbsp

- Beef base demi-glaze 1 tsp

- Rosemary sprig one.

- Freshly ground Black pepper to taste.

For the fondue.

- Eye round steak or filet mignon cut into ± 1-inch cubes.

- Vegetables of your choice (broccoli florets, mushrooms, bell peppers, etc.

- Additional sauces of your choice.

Procedure:

1. Heat the oil in a saucepan. When shimmering, sear the beef to give it color and establish the Maillard reactions. Set it aside for dipping.

2. Add onions and garlic sequentially in the same saucepan and oil and cook until translucent. Then, pour broth and red wine, stir well, and add Worcestershire sauce, beef semi-glaze, rosemary, and black pepper. Simmer for 5-7 minutes. Taste and correct seasonings if necessary.

3. Transfer the bouillon to the Fondue pot, set it to simmer, and serve immediately.

4. Dipping ingredients include seared beef, vegetables like broccoli, parboiled potato chunks, carrots, pickled turnips, cornichons, etc., and toasted bread cubes.

Seafood Fondue Inspired by (Pacific Seafood, n.d.)

For this dish, select crustaceans and shellfish that can be held in fondue forks. If using fish, choose a fish with substantial, meaty flesh that will not be lost in the pot.

There are two fondue liquid varieties: oil to fry the fondue dipping ingredients or fish stock or broth. The fondue broth can be served as a soup, adding residual fish, crustaceans, shellfish, and vegetables. Crabs, oysters, or fish with fragile flesh are not well suited for this preparation.

Ingredients for four servings:

- Fish filets ½ lb.
- Shelled lobster ½ lb.
- Peeled shrimp ½ lb.
- Sea Scallops dry, 15/lb. count preferably ½ lb.
- Vegetables of your choice.
- Oil 2 inches deep in the fondue pot.
- Salt 1 tsp

Procedure:

1. Cut seafood into bite-size pieces, ± 1 inch, and leave scallops whole.
2. Heat oil to 375°F, add salt to oil and place on fondue burner.
3. Each guest will cook to their liking.

Note: An alternate way of preparing this dish is using fish broth or stock instead of oil. Proceed the same way, and at the end of the meal, add residual ingredients and serve as a soup.

Chocolate Fondue. Inspired by (Cafe, 2007)

Ingredients for eight servings:

- ½ cup of heavy cream
- ½ cup of whole milk

- Two fingers, pinch of salt.

- Dark chocolate or chips. 12 oz

For dipping.

- Strawberries

- Banana chunks, 1-inch square

- Dried apricots.

- Apple or pear chunks.

- Cookies like Oreos, vanilla cookies, and Krispy Rice squares.

Procedure:

1. Heat the cream and milk to a slow simmer at medium heat.

2. Once simmering, remove from heat and add chocolate, whisking until smooth and incorporated.

3. Transfer to a heated fondue pot and serve.

Chocolate Coconut Fondue

Ingredients for four servings:

- Semi-sweet chocolate chopped   8 oz

- Evaporated milk or half and half   1/3 cup

- Tia Maria or 43 liquor   2 Tbsp

- Shredded, unsweetened, toasted coconut.   2 Tbsp

Procedure:

1. Toast the shredded coconut in an oven at 350°F for a couple of minutes, shake, and toast for another minute. Do not burn.

2. Melt the chocolate and milk in a double boiler, stirring until smooth. Remove from the heat, add the liquor, and stir. Transfer to the fondue pot over a burner to keep it warm, add coconut, and mix it well.

3. Serve immediately with chunks of pineapple, mango, apricot, bananas, and hard ladyfingers.

Soufflé

Soufflé is defined in Wikipedia as an egg-based dish originated in the Kingdom of France as it was known in the early seventeen hundreds. The noun soufflé comes from the verb souffler, which, translated into English, means to puff.

A souffle is prepared from two essential components: the base, a pastry sauce, bechamel sauce, or purée, and egg whites beaten to a soft peak (in a scrupulously clean bowl). The base provides the flavor, and the egg whites give the lift.

Basic Souffle (Get Cracking, n.d.)

Ingredients for four servings:

- Unsalted butter   2 Tbsp
- Flour, all-purpose   2 Tbsp
- Salt   ½ tsp
- Pepper   a pinch
- Hot milk   ¾ cup.
- Egg yolks   4
- Egg whites   5
- Cream of tartar   ¼ tsp

Procedure:

1. Preheat the oven to 375°F (190°C)

Prepare the base.

2. Make a roux by melting the butter and stirring the flour, salt, and pepper until the mixture is smooth and bubbly. Stir in the hot milk all at once. Continue stirring until boiling and the mixture is smooth and thickened (Bechamel).

3. Make the pastry cream by adding the yolks, tempered before, with some of the bechamel (1/4 cup) in aliquots. Once completed, set aside to cool some.

Prepare the lift.

4. Beat the cream of Tartar and the egg whites, preferably in a stand-up mixer, in a clean, large bowl until soft peaks form. Mix some of the egg whites into the base to lighten it up. Then, fold the mixture into the egg whites.

5. Prepare the vessel/s to bake the preparation. Butter the bottom and sides and dust with flour or sugar if it is a sweet pastry cream. Pour the preparation into a single souffle dish or individual ramekins.

6. Bake in the preheated oven at 375°F for 20-25 minutes or until puffed and lightly browned.

Note: You can flavor the base any way you wish, adding herbs or proteins like crab meat, cheese, shredded carrots, fruit purees, etc.

Classic Cheese and Leek Soufflé (Lemm, 2023)

Ingredients for six servings:

- Fat   Butter, unsalted 4 oz + enough to grease the souffle dish.

  Emmental cheese, grated 3 oz

  Milk 1 cup + 3 Tbsp

- Protein   Eggs, separated, four large.

- Carbohydrates   2 oz all-purpose flour

- Seasoning   Kosher salt and freshly ground pepper to taste.

- Flavor   Dijon Mustard 2 tsp
- Produce   Leek, medium, cleaned white parts cubed small 1.

Procedure:

1. Preheat the oven to 395°F (200°C) and prep all ingredients (Mise en place).

Prepare the base:

2. Melt the butter on medium-low heat. Add the leeks and cook until soft. Warm the milk.

3. *Make a roux and flavor it.* Add the flour and mustard, stirring; do not brown the roux.

4. *Make a bechamel.* Add the warm milk, stirring continuously to avoid lumps. The sauce should be thick and glossy; season with salt and pepper.

5. *Make a pastry sauce.* Add the egg yolks (temper them with some bechamel first) and mix well with a spatula or wooden spoon, ensuring they are well incorporated.

6. Add the grated cheese to complete the base's flavor, stirring until all the cheese is melted.

7. *Prepare the lift: Beat the egg whites using a stand-up mixer until they are firm and form peaks like bird beaks.*

8. *Lighten the base.* Mix 2 Tbsp of the beaten egg whites to the base. Then, fold the lightened base into the egg whites, preserving their volume.

9. In the previously buttered and dusted with flour, carefully and gently spoon the soufflé mixture into the

soufflé dish or individual dishes, making sure you have at least 1 inch to the top. Otherwise, place a parchment paper collar.

10. Bake in the preheated oven until golden brown on the surface (± 15 minutes)

Goat Cheese Soufflé with Glazed Oranges and Apples or Pears. Inspired by (Bird, n.d.)

Ingredients for 6-8 servings:

- Protein   Eggs, large, separated 7.

- Carbohydrates   Flour, all-purpose 22Tbsp

- Fat   Unsalted butter 2 sticks + 6 Tbsp

  Cheese parmesan, grated ¾ cup. (2.65 oz)

  Goat Cheese 2.65 oz

- Liquid   Milk Whole, 3 cups.

  Port wine 1 cup

  Balsamic vinegar ¼ cup

- Seasoning   Kosher salt 1 ½ tsp level.

- Fruit   Apple one in thin slices.

  Orange supreme

Procedure:

1. Reduce 1 cup of port and ¼ cup of balsamic vinegar while poaching apple slices cut thin in a mandolin. Add supreme orange segments and simmer for three more minutes when the mix becomes syrupy. Set aside.

2. ***Make the Bechamel*** by heating to simmer the 3 cups of milk and preparing the roux by melting the butter and adding the flour and salt. When all the flour is incorporated, add the warm milk immediately, stirring constantly to avoid lumps. Set aside to cool to 140°F. This is the base.

3. ***Add the flavor to the base,*** melt the cheese into the base, temper the yolks with some of the base, and then add them. This is a pastry sauce. Set it aside.

4. ***Prepare the lift.*** In a stand-up mixer, whisk the egg whites to stiff peaks. Lighten the base by mixing 2-3 Tbsp of the egg whites. Then, fold the base into the egg whites, transfer to a prepared soufflé dish (buttered and dusted), and bake at 350°F (175°C) for 15-20 minutes. It should have risen and been golden brown on the top.

5. Serve immediately. Top them with glazed apples and orange wedges supreme.

Quinoa Soufflé

I learned this recipe from a chef at the Inka-terra Hotel in Machu Pichu, Cuzco Perú.

Ingredients for 4-6 servings:

- Protein   Quinoa cooked, any type or combinations of 2 cups.

  Eggs, large, separated, four.

- Carbohydrates   Breadcrumbs 2 Tbsp

  Flour, all-purpose, unbleached 2. Tbsp

- Fat   Butter, unsalted 2 Tbsp

  Cheese, Gouda, or Gruyere, shredded, 4 oz

- Seasoning   Kosher salt ½ tsp, white pepper ¼ tsp

- Flavoring   Nutmeg, freshly grated one pinch.

- Liquid   Milk, hot, 1 cup.

Procedure:

1. Preheat the oven to 375°F. Butter the bottom and sides of the fondue dish or individual ramekins and sprinkle with breadcrumbs.

2. Wash and cook the quinoa. Wash to eliminate bitterness; I like to cook quinoa like rice pilaf. First, toast the quinoa briefly in a saucepan with a bit of butter, salt, and minced garlic, then add water at a 1.5:1 ratio and boil the mixture until the surface of the quinoa is visible. Then cover partially, lower the heat to low, and cook until it is done.

Grains should be separated and have the consistency of cooked rice. Fluff it with a fork, ready to be used in the souffle.

Make the Base.

3. Heat the milk to simmer and simultaneously prepare the roux.

4. *Prepare the Roux: Melt the butter (medium-low heat), add the flour progressively while stirring with a wooden spoon, and cook until foamy—do not let it brown; it should be pale yellow. Add the hot milk (off the heat), stirring to incorporate. Return to the heat, boil,* and cook at medium heat until thickened (*Bechamel*). Add the seasonings and nutmeg.

5. *Make a sort of pastry cream (no sugar) by tempering the egg yolks with a Tbsp of the bechamel at a time for 3-4 times. Then,* mix the egg yolks in the bechamel and flavor *the base* by melting the cheese in the preparation and adding the quinoa. Empty the base into a large mixing bowl and set aside.

6. *Prepare the lift.* Whisk the egg whites until foamy in a separate bowl, preferably in a stand mixer (make sure it is spotless); whisk them until frothy. Add a two-finger pinch of salt and 1/8 tsp of cream of tartar. Gradually increase the speed until stiff peaks form.

7. *Lighten the base* by adding and stirring ¼ of the egg whites into the base. Then, gently fold in the rest of the egg whites.

8. Pour the souffle mixture into the prepared mold/s, place the soufflé mold in the oven, and bake until puffed and

golden brown (30-35 minutes). Turn the heat off and leave in the oven for another 5 minutes. Serve immediately. You may use a cream-diluted cilantro paste as a serving sauce.

Quinoa and Cheese Soufflé

Dulce de Leche Soufflé.

I learned this recipe from a chef in Bariloche, Argentina. When I visited, he graciously invited me to his kitchen and showed me how to make the dish.

Ingredients for six servings:

For Béchamel

- 2/3 c. whole milk or 1 ½ cups of Half and Half instead of milk and cream.

- 2/3 c. cream

- 1 ½ Tbsp all-purpose flour

271

- 1 ½ Tbsp corn starch

- 7Tbsp + ½ tsp of butter

For Pastry sauce

- five egg yolks

- 1/3 c. sugar

- 150 g of dulce de leche

For the lift. Egg whites

- seven egg whites

- 2Tbsp of sugar

- 1/8 tsp cream of tartar.

PROCEDURE

Make the base.

1. Prepare *a white roux* with butter, flour, and cornstarch. Add the hot milk and cream to create the Béchamel when a nutty aroma is present. Keep warm.

2. Prepare the *pastry cream* by whisking the egg yolks and sugar until pale, then add the dulce de leche while still mixing (*pastry cream*).

3. Temper the egg yolk mix with a tablespoon at a time of the hot béchamel, still mixing with the whisk, repeat for 6 Tbsp of béchamel into the egg mix.

4. Then fold the egg mix into the remaining béchamel and cook for a few minutes until the cream thickens; keep warm or refrigerate if prepared early (*this is the Base*).

5. ***Prepare the lift.*** Beat the egg whites and add sugar. While beating, add a pinch of salt and 1 tsp of tartar cream until they form stiff peaks when the whisk is lifted.

6. Lighten the yolk mix with two tablespoons of beaten egg whites.

7. Mix the yolk into the beaten egg whites and pour into a soufflé dish pre-greased with butter and sprinkled with confectioners' sugar. You may put a parchment paper collar outside using egg whitewash and a string.

8. Bake at 350° for 15 to 18 minutes. It should be puffed up and golden brown. Remove, dust with confectioners' sugar, and serve immediately.

9. You may use a cream Anglaise + dulce de leche to pour over when serving.

Soufflé of Carob Syrup.

This is a dish from Northern Perú. It uses the syrup of the Algarrobo tree (Carob) and is like dulce de leche soufflé.

Ingredients for six servings:

For Béchamel

- 2/3 c. whole milk   or 1 ½ cups of half and half

- 2/3 c. cream

- 1 ½ Tbsp all-purpose flour

- 1 ½ Tbsp corn starch

- 7.12 Tbsp butter

For Pastry sauce

- five egg yolks

- 1/3 c. sugar

- 150 g of Carob syrup.

For the lift. Egg whites

- seven egg whites

- 2 Tbsp of sugar

- 1/8 tsp cream of tartar.

- one pinch of salt (2 finger pinch).

For the sauce

- Heavy cream ½ cup.

- Carob syrup 2 Tbsp

Procedure:

1. **Prepare pastry cream:** Beat egg yolks with sugar and flour. Heat the milk and add it to the yolk mixture (Temper the egg yolks first). Bring to the fire and cook at low heat while mixing with a wooden spoon until the cream thickens (5 minutes). Remove and let warm.

2. ***Make the Base.*** Add the Carob syrup (*flavor*) to the pastry cream. Mix well (This is the Base)

3. ***Prepare the lift***. Beat the egg whites with a pinch of salt. Incorporate them in the preparation of the base with wrapping movements.

4. Pour the mixture into the buttered mold, dusted with sugar (or use the individual molds). Bring to the oven and cook at a moderate temperature, 375°F (190°C), for about 20 minutes, until the soufflé is puffed and golden brown.

5. ***Garnish*** with banana and heavy cream with carob syrup.

6. Remove the soufflé and serve it right away.

CHAPTER 14

Sauces, Dressings, and Herb Pastes

We will begin this chapter with Base preparations since they are used as a base for so many dishes. We will then follow with the classical Mother French sauces and derivate sauces from each mother sauce.

Base Preparations

Many dishes begin with a base preparation and, depending on how you use them for broths, soups, or stews, you cut the ingredients in cubes, larger for soups or smaller for braises or stews. You cook them with small amounts of fat, the cooking should be done slowly at medium-low heat (low and slow). You sweat the vegetables on low heat for a long time and then add a liquid to deglaze the pan (wine, broth, or water), in the amount and kind, depending on the dish you want to prepare.

- **_Mirepoix_** is made with fat, usually butter and vegetables: 2 parts onions, 1 part carrots, and 1 part celery by weight, diced small to increase the surface and produce faster cooking. The vegetables should become soft and transparent.

- ***Holy Trinity*** is the Cajun version of the mirepoix, but in it, carrots are replaced by green peppers. The vegetable ratio can be equal parts of all three ingredients or two parts onions and 1 part each of celery and green pepper. The fat is usually olive oil.

- ***Pinçage*** is like mirepoix, but it is cooked until it turns brown but not burned black, and then tomato paste is added. While mirepoix adds a clean, fresh vegetable complexity to your food, Pinçage is more assertive and has a strong presence. It is an excellent way to amp up the flavor of stews and braises or to use on rice or quinoa salads, essentially enhancing umami.

- ***Soffrito*** is a vegetable mix that varies in different regions, such as Puerto Rican, which uses sweet red peppers, tomato concasse, onions, garlic, culantro or cilantro, and yellow pepper. In Perú, it is called **aderezo** and uses onions, garlic, and ají amarillo.

- ***Ratatouille Sauce*** (≈ **caponata**) is a base preparation of creole origin, and it uses in a 1:1 ratio of yellow onion, green bell pepper, a small eggplant, and a medium zucchini, all diced. Add four minced garlic cloves, salt, and black pepper to taste, ½ tsp of sugar, ¼ tsp of Cajun spices, 15 oz of tomato puree (15 oz), 1 tsp Balsamic vinegar and 3 Tbsp water. In a large skillet, cook the onions and bell pepper low and slow in olive oil until the onions are translucent and bell peppers are soft, about 6-7 minutes. Add the eggplant, zucchini, garlic, salt, pepper, sugar, and Cajun spices. Reduce the heat to medium-low and cook for 15 minutes, stirring occasionally. Add the tomatoes, vinegar, and water.

Simmer covered for about 15 more minutes, stirring occasionally. Serve over pasta or rice or as a salad.

- **_The caponata_** dish from Sicily is remarkably similar. In addition to the Ratatouille sauce, olives, and oregano are added _and_ served as a salad.

- **_Aderezo_** is the Peruvian base version, prepared by cooking low and slow onions cubed small, garlic (pressed), chili paste, amarillo, or red pepper –Rocoto.

French Mother Sauces

These are called mother sauces because they are the origin of many different sauces. They are prepared by adding a liquid to a thickening agent. (Delhindra, 2019)

Table 4: French Mother Sauces

NAME	LIQUID	THICKENING AGENT
Béchamel	milk	**white roux** **(butter + flour)**
Veloute	white stock	**white roux** **(butter + flour)**
Espagnole	brown stock	**brown roux +** **tomato paste**
Tomato sauce	tomato puree	**roux or** **reduction of tomato puree**
Hollandaise	clarified butter	**egg yolks**

The sauces should be thick, smothering, or clinging to whatever is drizzled, dolloped, or poured. This consistency is accomplished by thickening agents like roux, reduction like in tomato sauce, or emulsification like in Hollandaise sauce.

How to make a roux: Its two ingredients are fat (butter, ghee, or coconut oil) and all-purpose flour in a 1:1 ratio by weight. If you use 3 ounces of each, this ratio will thicken a quart of liquid (milk, stock). An ounce of all-purpose flour is about 3½ Tbsp, and an ounce of butter is 2 Tbsp

Melt the butter in a saucepan (remember, melted butter melts butter best) and add the flour progressively, stirring and cooking until you get a nutty aroma, indicating the flour is cooked (several minutes). The longer you cook, the darker it will get (yellow-golden to brown and dark brown), but it will also lose its thickening power. Be careful not to burn it.

To prepare the sauce, add the liquid progressively (to avoid lumps), let it boil, and then turn off the heat when the desired thickness is achieved. You will be left with a thick, creamy, warm mix.

Mother sauces

Béchamel sauce

It is a versatile sauce that could be used in casseroles, as a base for savory soufflés, and with other ingredients, such as pasta or mac and cheese. (Saulnier, 1982)

Ingredients

6 cups milk or nondairy milk

2 oz (4 Tbsp) ghee or clarified butter.

2 oz (7 Tbsp) all-purpose flour

Procedure

1. Warm the milk to avoid splattering when adding to the roux.

2. Make the roux as above and Cook to get the nutty aroma (blond roux).

3. Add the warm milk and a couple of Tbsp First, stir with a whisk; when it is not lumpy, add the rest, whisk continuously, and cook until thick and creamy.

Veloute sauce

This includes chicken, veal, or fish Veloute sauce. It is not usually used as a finished sauce, even though it could be used as a gravy after seasoning it with salt and pepper. I like adding Peruvian ají amarillo (yellow pepper). The Veloute sauce is often used as a base for many derivatives. The following recipe is used because of the white wine with fish, and the base is Veloute. (Saulnier, 1982)

Procedure:

1. Warm the fish stock and keep warm (6 cups).

2. Prepare the roux as above using 4 Tbsp clarified butter (2 oz) and 7 Tbsp flour (2 oz). Cook until the nutty aroma emerges (blond roux).

3. Progressively add the warm fish stock, whisking vigorously until it is free of lumps. Simmer until it has reduced by 1/3, stirring so it will not Burn on the bottom of the pan.

4. Remove the pan from the heat source and pour the sauce through a wire mesh lined with cheesecloth.

5. Cover the sauce surface with plastic wrap to avoid forming skin.

Hollandaise Sauce (Saulnier, 1982) *alternate* ***(unknown, blogs/recipes/hollandaise-sauce)***

It is often used on Eggs Benedict, asparagus, salmon, and filet mignon, sometimes with added ingredients like chili sauce.

Ingredients for two servings:

4 Tbsp butter

4 egg yolks

2 Tbsp fresh lime juice

1 Tbsp heavy cream

Salt and pepper to taste

Procedure:

1. Melt the butter in a small saucepan or a double boiler, but do not let it brown.

2. Beat the egg yolks, lime juice, heavy cream, salt, and pepper in a bowl.

3. Temper the egg yolk mixture one teaspoon at a time with the warm butter up to 15 teaspoons (5 tablespoons).

4. Pour the egg yolk mixture into the melted butter, turn the heat low, whisk vigorously, and cook for 10-15 seconds. If it is still too runny, cook a few more seconds until the consistency is to your liking.

5. Serve immediately.

Tomato Sauce

It is used often with spaghetti, pizza, and other uses like shakshuka. 4 (eggs cooked in tomato sauce) (STEPHENS, 2021)

Ingredients and Procedure:

1. Big 4: garlic, olive oil, San Marzano tomatoes, basil

2. Mash up tomatoes using a potato masher.

3. Salt liberally to counter acid.

4. Use a cast iron skillet for preparing sauce.

5. Use sugar to counter bitterness, a pinch, or a tsp of brown sugar.

6. Pasta: remove from boiling water 2 minutes shy of al dente. Finish it in the sauce mix and cover it.

7. Add a cup of the pasta water to the tomato sauce before adding the pasta.

8. Use dry herbs and spices (dry oregano, dry basil, and dry parsley). You may consider adding cumin, coriander, and ají).

9. Do not forget the dairy (cheese, for meats except chicken or fish).

10. Add wine and simmer to half the amount.

11. Add natural acids like lemon, capers, and olives if the sauce is bland.

12. Balance the pasta with the sauce. The thicker the pasta, the more acid it needs to be balanced.

13. Add more flavor to the sauce with EVOO at this point.

14. Slow-cook the sauce, preferably in a pressure cooker over low heat, for 4 hours before adding the pasta. The sauce can be made a day or two ahead.

15. Just before serving, add fresh chopped basil (use an extra sharp knife, and don't press hard on the rolled-up leaves to avoid bruising the basil). To chop the basil, roll up the leaves, cut across to the desired thickness, and cut them in opposite directions once.

16. Instead of grated Parmesan, consider shaved Parmesan on the side.

Espagnole sauce (Fosil Farms)

It is a basic brown sauce that is the starting point for a demi-glace, a rich and deep-flavored sauce used mostly with red meats. It is like Veloute sauce in that it is a stock-based sauce (beef stock in this case), and the thickening agent is roux (brown in this case). It has additional ingredients: tomato paste and mirepoix. (Saulnier, 1982)

Ingredients for eight servings:

Bay leaf

1/2 tsp dried thyme

3 to 4 fresh parsley stems

7 to 8 whole black peppercorns

1 oz clarified butter

1/2 cup onions (diced)

1/4 cup carrots (diced)

1/4 cup celery (diced)

7 Tbsp all-purpose flour

3 cups brown stock (i.e., beef stock) unsalted

2 Tbsp tomato purée

Procedure:

1. Gather the ingredients.

2. Fold the bay leaf, thyme, parsley stems, and peppercorns in a square of cheesecloth and tie the corners with a piece of kitchen twine. Leave the string long enough to tie it to the handle of your pot to make it easier to retrieve.

3. In a heavy-bottomed saucepan, melt the butter over medium heat until it becomes frothy.

4. Add the mirepoix—onions, carrots, and celery—and sauté for a few minutes until it is lightly browned. Do not Let it burn, though.

5. With a wooden spoon, stir the flour into the mirepoix until it is fully incorporated and forms a thick paste (this is your roux).

6. Lower the heat and cook the roux for another 5 minutes until it starts to take on a noticeably light brown color. Again, do not Let it burn.

7. Using a wire whisk, slowly add the stock and tomato purée to the roux, whisking vigorously to make sure it is free of lumps.

8. Bring to a boil, lower the heat, add the sachet, and simmer (Alfaro, 2019) for about 50 minutes or until the total volume has reduced by about one-third, stirring frequently to ensure the sauce does not scorch at the bottom of the pan.

9. Use a spoon to skim off any impurities that rise to the surface.

10. Remove the sauce from the heat and retrieve the sachet.

11. carefully pour the sauce through a wire mesh strainer lined with cheesecloth for a smooth consistency.

12. If you will not be serving the sauce immediately, keep it covered and warm until you are ready to use it.

13. Otherwise, serve hot and enjoy!

Roasted beef with Espagnole sauce

You can use store-bought beef stock to make your Espagnole, but as always, make sure to use low-sodium or, if possible, unsalted stock. Anytime you Reduce a liquid with salt in it; concentrating the saltiness might not be a good idea, especially if you plan to use the resulting sauce to make yet another sauce, which might be reduced. It's better to season at the very end of cooking.

Derivatives of Mother Sauces (Delhindra, 2019) (Saulnier, 1982)

The mother sauces have many derivatives, too many for this simple cookbook. I will try to present them in as simplified a way as I can and, at the same time, provide enough information so you can create them to your taste or maybe create your new sauce.

Béchamel Derivatives

Mornay Sauce: Its origin is the Béchamel; adding grated Parmesan and Gruyere cheeses requires no additional reduction. It is used in pasta and lasagna. Ingredients: Bechamel: 1 quart. Warm it with an onion and two whole cloves, then remove. Add two ounces each of grated Gruyere and Parmesan. Serve immediately.

Herb Sauce: Its origin is the Béchamel; adding herbs of your choice requires no additional reduction. It is used in pasta, casseroles, and gratins.

Mustard sauce: It originates from the Béchamel, adding prepared mustard, no shallots, and no additional reduction needed; it is used with vegetables, eggs, chicken, and casseroles.

Lobster sauce: its origin is from Béchamel, adding anchovy paste, diced lobster meat, ají. No additional reduction is needed; it is used with all types of seafood.

Cream Sauce: Its origin is from Béchamel. It adds heavy cream; no additional reduction is needed. It is used in sandwiches like Croque Monsieur and others.

Nantua sauce is a classic seafood sauce that incorporates shrimp butter and cream into a bechamel sauce. The ingredients are bechamel, 1 quart, shrimp butter, 6 Tbsp, and heavy cream ½ cups.

Soubise sauce is a classic cream sauce that adds sauté onions to butter. The ratio is onions, one lb. per cream sauce, 1 quart.

Crème Anglaise is a sweet custard-like sauce. Prepare a bechamel and separately mix the egg yolks with sugar. Heat the milk and cream, temper the egg yolk mixture, and mix them while stirring (pastry sauce). When this pastry sauce is tempered and combined with the bechamel, you have the base for a soufflé when folded into whipped egg whites.

Veloute Derivatives

Supreme sauce: It originates from Veloute Chicken, adding cream. No additional reduction is needed; it is used with specially poached poultry.

White wine sauce: its origin is Veloute fish. Additional ingredients include white wine with additional reduction at this point, adding the cream, butter, salt, and pepper. It is used primarily with seafood.

Normandy Sauce: Its origin is Velouté fish, with additional ingredients (in equal volume as the velouté fish) of mushroom liquor if using dried mushrooms and mussels' liquor or fish stock. Reduce by half, add the cream and (4 Tbsp) butter in pieces until the desired consistency is achieved. You may use a combination of butter and egg yolks for liaison.

Sauce Bercy: Its origin is the Veloute fish, with additional ingredients of white wine, shallots minced with additional reduction at this point to ½, then add butter 4 Tbsp by pieces until desired consistency, flavor with salt, pepper, and other spices of your choice. It is used primarily with poached fish.

Mushroom sauce: for fish, its origin is Veloute fish with additional mushrooms, reduce by ½, and add a liaison of egg yolks and heavy cream to the desired consistency. It is used primarily for fish and crustaceans.

Sauce Allemande or Parisienne: Its origin is Veloute veal. The additional ingredients include cream, egg yolks, lemon juice, salt, and pepper. No further reduction is necessary. It is used for eggs, poached chicken, veal, and vegetables.

Mushroom sauce for poultry originated in the Allemande sauce with additional mushrooms, so no further reduction is needed. It is used for poultry.

Bonnefoy or white bordelaise originates from the Veloute sauce for fish or chicken. Add Bay leaf and pepper thyme, reduce to half, add the white Bordeaux wine and shallots, and reduce by half again. It is used for chicken, fish, shrimp, and lobster.

Sauce Indene: its origin is Veloute chicken, fish, and veal. Additional ingredients include curry powder, coconut cream or milk, lemon juice, or curry paste. Reduce the mix to the desired consistency. It can be used with any protein depending on the velouté used, and you can add potatoes or other vegetables.

Espagnole Derivatives

Sauce Bordelaise: Its origin is Espagnole sauce, with red wine, shallots, and beef demi glaze. While reducing in process, add bay leaf, thyme, and pepper. Begin by slowly cooking the shallots in butter. When caramelized, add the wine. Lower the temperature and let it simmer until the wine is almost evaporated. Add the Espagnole sauce or veal stock and cook until reduced by ½. Pour the sauce through a conical fine mesh strainer to the last few drops—season with salt and black pepper.

Sauce Bourguignonne: Its origin is in the Espagnole sauce. Begin the process by slowly cooking the shallots in clarified butter. Add the red wine and cook until almost evaporated. Then add the Espagnole sauce and some chilies if you prefer. Cook to the desired consistency.

Sauce Diable: Its origin is the Espagnole sauce. It needs additional reduction by adding white wine and shallots. It is used in grilled chicken or pigeons.

Sauce lyonnaise: Its origin is the Espagnole sauce. It begins with browning the onions and needs additional reduction to the added white wine, vinegar, and Espagnole sauce. It is used in roasted meats, pork, poultry, and sausages.

Madeira sauce: Its origin is the Espagnole sauce. The added Madeira needs to be reduced to the desired consistency. It is used in roasted meats and steaks.

Perigueux sauce: Its origins are in the Espagnole sauce, which has added truffles and truffle pâté. It needs no additional reduction and is used in roasted meats and steaks.

Sauce Bercy (Brown): Its origin is the Espagnole sauce. It begins by cooking the shallots in butter and crushed peppercorns. The added white wine requires an additional reduction. It is used for grilled meats.

Tomato Sauce Derivatives

Portuguese sauce: Its origin is tomato sauce. It needs an additional reduction of the tomato sauce with added Tomato concasse, meat glaze, parsley, olives, anchovies, chopped onions, garlic, salt, and sugar. It is used in sautéed fish that is then simmered in the sauce.

Milanese Sauce: Its origin is tomato sauce. Further reduction is needed for added beef demi glaze. It begins with small, cubed onions, garlic pressed, and julienned mushrooms until soft. Then, add all the other ingredients and cook low and slow. It is used in pasta, chicken, and pounded and breaded beef.

Hollandaise Sauce Derivatives

Sauce mousseline, or Chantilly, originates from Hollandaise sauce. It consists of mixing 2/3 of Hollandaise with 1/3 of whipped heavy cream. It is used in steamed or poached fish, asparagus, or broccoli.

Sauce Bavarois: Its origins are in the Hollandaise sauce. An additional reduction is needed for the added crayfish butter and tails. It is used on fish.

Sauce Rubens: Its origins are in the hollandaise sauce. It will need an additional reduction. Begin by reducing white wine, fish stock, and fine mirepoix. Strain and add the yolk of eggs and crayfish butter to finish.

Béarnaise sauce: It originated with Hollandaise sauce. It begins with a reduction of chopped shallots, mignonette peppercorns, tarragon, salt, and vinegar. Then add the egg yolks and melted butter, whisking briskly on low fire to ensure the yolks get cooked, and strain through a cheesecloth-covered strainer. Finally, add chopped tarragon and chervil. It is like hollandaise, but the acid used is vinegar instead of lemon Juice.

Francoise sauce originates from the béarnaise, with added fish glaze and tomato puree. It is used on fish and pasta.

Modern Sauces

Chef Jacob Burton in his Stella Culinary Boot Camp ((Stella Culinary Chef Jacob's, n.d.) Introduces the concept of 3 methods to produce or create sauces: reduction, emulsification, and puree.

We have already reviewed the mother French sauces, and as you can imagine, remembering them and derivate sauces is daunting. They are primarily based on some liquid (stock, milk) and roux (white to brown).

The approach favored by ***Chef Jacob Burton is attractive because it concentrates on the methods of producing sauces, allowing you to develop proficiency quickly and*** create sauces according to your flavor preferences.

I will limit myself to giving a glimpse of these methods, but I encourage all to review his videos and podcasts.

Reduction Method:

Two reasons to reduce a sauce are to thicken it and intensify flavors.

There are two types of stocks: white and brown. The difference is that in brown stocks, the bones have been roasted; in white stocks, they have not. Therefore, there will be white and brown sauces. Depending on the bones used, they can be vegetables, veal, lamb, chicken, or fish.

The time required to simmer the stock preparation varies from 8-12 hours for veal or lamb to 45-60 minutes for fish stocks.

Knuckles, short ribs, and neck bones (bone marrow-rich) are preferred for veal or lamb.

Then, these stocks undergo a process of reinforcement and reduction to prepare the sauce. Reinforcement is accomplished by preparing a mirepoix in beef fat (butter?) at medium-low heat. When caramelizing is ready enough to deglaze the fond with wine (white for white stocks, red wine for brown stocks), reduce the wine by ½- 2/3, then add the stock and simmer by ½ again. This is a demiglace.

Now, it can be used to prepare a sauce like a pan sauce, for example, after having seared a filet and roasted it in the pan in an oven to the degree of doneness desired. You then rest the filet and, in the meantime, prepare the sauce with the fond in the pan, discarding the excess fat, sauteing some shallots, and when the shallots are beginning to brown, add wine and reduce by half or 3/4. Then, add the demiglace and another reduction to get to the desired thickness and flavor intensity, reaching the nape stage (cover the back of a spoon and leave a track when wiped with a fingertip).

At this stage, you may add any flavor desired and a bit of butter, and to round things up, add a drop or two of lime juice or vinegar.

Emulsion Method

An Emulsion is the product of mixing two substances that are not soluble in each other. It is formed by suspending tiny droplets of one substance into the other. Emulsions tend to be unstable, meaning they tend to separate into layers. The mixing is accomplished by shaking them so the droplets become smaller and can be suspended (Dispersed phase). They separate when the substances' agitation (shearing power) stops.

The most common culinary emulsions are milk, cream, and butter in their natural state. Why are they stable? They contain substances that have polar molecules, with one pole soluble in water and the other pole soluble in fat, making the emulsion stable. A typical example of this mechanism is amino acids (proteins). Another mechanism is Phospholipids like lecithin. Egg yolks contain both mechanisms, lecithin and proteins, so they are used in the preparations of emulsions such as Hollandaise sauce, Mayonnaise, and aioli.

Other substances also stabilize emulsions that work primarily by increasing viscosity, such as proteins, starches, pectin, and food gums. Some will work only in hot emulsions, while others gums will work in cold or hot emulsions.

To obtain a suitable emulsion, it is necessary to apply the shearing power to the dispersant (water, vinegar, etc.) with small amounts of the dispersed substance (fats) so the dispersed droplets can become the smallest possible, then add fat slowly until the suitable emulsion is obtained, as the emulsion forms the fat can be added faster. The more fat is added, the thicker the emulsion will be.

Sauces of Different Origins

In addition to these many sauces, there are numerous by ethnic and regional groups and by their era. Examples are in a book titled Modern Sauces (Holmberg, 2012), where you will find a recipe for "Caramelized Onions Coulis," which is prepared with caramelized onions, a reduction of crème fraiche, broth, and some acid from lemon juice.

Some examples of regional sauces (not French) that are of everyday use.

Huancaína Sauce

This sauce originates from the Andean city of Huancayo in Perú.

Sauce based on farmer cheese, ají amarillo (contrasting flavors, Rule 2), unified by cream and oil.

Ingredients for six servings:

- ½ cup Ají amarillo paste
- 2 Tbsp vegetable oil (canola or grape seed oil)
- ½ cup heavy cream or half and half
- ½ lb. farmers' cheese soaked in milk to reduce saltiness
- Soda or water crackers (optional) cracked ¼ cup or less for thickening.

Procedure:

1. Place all ingredients in a food processor or blender.'

2. Process until smooth. Refrigerate until ready to use.

It can be used in various ways, including as a dipping sauce for French fries, fried yucca (cassava), pasta, risotto, and, traditionally, over-boiled potatoes with an Alfonso olive and a slice of hardboiled egg.

Huancaina Potatoes

Tamarind sauce

Ingredients for eight servings:

- Tamarind 12 pods.

- Water (1/2 cup + 2 Tbsp (150 ml).

- Sugar 2 oz + tsp (60 g.)

- White wine vinegar 2 Tbsp

Procedure:

1. The first step is to clean the tamarind pulp from their pods, open the pod and remove the shell of hard skin, the pits are chained by a string, remove it. Then open each of the segments and remove the seeds.

2. Only the pulp of the fruit is left. Place it in a saucepan with warm water and soak it for 5 minutes.

3. . Then bring them to the stove and, at medium heat, stirring constantly, dissolve the pulp in the water, then add the sugar and vinegar.

4. You may add ají paste, tomato paste, or another flavoring of your choice. The tamarind's natural flavor is intense and acidic.

5. Place the mixture in a blender, pulse 5-7 times, then strain through a fine mesh strainer. If it is too dense, add a bit of hot water; if it is too watery, add a slurry of cornstarch to thicken it.

It can be used to puree vegetables, as part of salad dressings, or as an ingredient in simmering liquids for meats, poultry, or fish. If you double the sugar, the sauce will be sweet and sour.

Example Recipe for Use of Tamarind Sauce

Pork Tenderloin Medallions in Tamarind Sauce

Ingredients for two servings:

- Pork Tenderloin 1 lb.

- Tamarind sauce

- Onion red small, sliced thick.

- Coconut milk 1 ¾ cups.

- Dried apricots six.

- Raisins 1 Tbsp

- Olive oil extra virgin.

- Salt and pepper to taste.

Procedure:

1. Sear the meat and cut the tenderloin into slices ½-inch thick, using extra virgin olive oil. When shimmering, add the pork medallions and sear both sides lightly. Reserve the medallions on a platter.

2. In the same skillet with residual oil, cook the onions until translucent; stir the bottom to use any residual funds. When the onions begin to acquire some golden color, add the coconut milk and stir.

3. Add the raisins and dried apricots (rehydrated in lukewarm water) and return the pork medallions. Reserve and simmer for 5 minutes.

4. Add 3 tbsp of tamarind sauce and simmer for another 5 minutes, stirring to allow all the flavors to meld.

5. Serve over roasted potatoes or rice pilaf.

Tamarillo and Ají sauce

Tamarillo is a fruit from South America, also known as the tomato tree because it resembles tomatoes. There are two varieties, red and orange, and both flavors are similar. You can obtain the pulp of the fruit from internet-based vendors.

Ingredients for six servings:

- Vegetable oil neutral flavor   2Tbsp
- Ají Amarillo paste   3Tbsp
- Onion, white, small   cubed small
- Garlic cloves, large, two minced or pressed.
- Tamarillo pulp   6 Tbsp
- Olive oil   ½ cup
- Salt and Pepper to taste

Procedure:

1. In a skillet, sauté the onions and ají amarillo paste. When the onions are soft, add the pressed garlic, stirring to avoid burning the garlic. Remove from the heat.

2. In a blender, mix the tamarillo pulp, olive oil,

3. and the sauté onions. Pulse a few times until homogeneous.

You can simmer seared protein (chicken or fish) in the sauce and serve it with rice or potatoes.

Salsa Macha

Salsa Macha is a Mexican salsa based on chilis, nuts, sugar, and vinegar. The version I am presenting is a variation using Peruvian chilies. I replaced the brown sugar with stevia (to keep the sugar load small) and added 1 tsp of molasses for the flavor.

Ingredients for eight servings:

- Carbohydrates — Brown sugar 1 Tbsp or 1 Tbsp of stevia + 1 tsp molasses.

- Fat — 1 ½ cup of olive oil

- Nuts and seeds — ½ cup of raw macadamia.
  Sesame seeds 2 Tbsp

- Aromatics — Onion, red, medium, cubed small one onion.
  Garlic cloves, large 4 pressed.
  Ají Amarillo paste 2 Tbsp
  Ají Panca paste 2 Tbsp

- Seasoning — Kosher salt 1 tsp or to taste.

- Liquid — Distilled white vinegar 3 Tbsp

Procedure:

1. In a large skillet with a heavy bottom, heat the oil to shimmering but not smoking. Add the onions; when softening, add the garlic, stirring to avoid burning the garlic and giving it a bitter taste.

2. Quickly add the macadamia nuts, keeping a close eye because they will go from browning to burning quickly. Add the sesame seeds and the Ají pastes, cook for a minute or two to toast the ají paste, and remove from the heat.

3. Transfer all the contents of the skillet to a blender or food processor. Add the sugar, stevia, molasses, brown stevia, salt, and vinegar, and process until smooth.

4. If not being used immediately, Place in a vacuum container and refrigerate. Reheat before using.

Chimichurri Sauce

The origin of the name is unclear. The sauce originated in Argentina and has spread through Latin America. It is now not rare to find it in the USA at restaurants and supermarkets. It is packed with aromatics and herbs balanced through olive oil and vinegar.

Ingredients for eight servings:

- Fat   Extra virgin olive oil ½ cup

- Aromatics and Herbs cloves.   Garlic, five medium-large

  Parsley leaves, fresh 1 cup packed.

  Oregano leaves 2 Tbsp

- Seasoning   Kosher salt 1 tsp

  Ají Amarillo powder ¼ tsp

- Liquid (acid)   Red wine vinegar ¼ cup

Procedure:

1. place the parsley, oregano, and garlic in a food processor and pulse until finely chopped.

2. Transfer to a medium bowl and whisk by hand (to minimize oxidation) the oil, vinegar, salt, and ají.

3. Use immediately or place in a vacuum container and refrigerate for a few days.

Note: a variation includes cilantro leaves (cilantro ½ cup and ½ cup of parsley).

Gremolata

This is an Italian Parsley lemon oil like chimichurri).

Ingredients for four servings:

- Fat   ½ cup olive oil extra virgin.

- Aromatics   Garlic 2 cloves large, peeled.

  Parsley leaves 1 cup, packed.

  Ají Amarillo powder, a two-finger pinch.

- Liquid (acid)   Lemon Zest of 1 small lemon and lemon juice 2 tsp

- Seasoning   Kosher salt and black pepper freshly ground to taste.

Procedure:

1. Place garlic and zest in a food processor and pulse until chopped.

2. Add oil, salt, pepper, and lemon juice. If you want a little heat, add the ají amarillo. Pulse to mix.

3. Store in a vacuum container refrigerated for up to a week.

Notes: It can be used in almost any dish, including soups, stews, fish, shellfish, pasta, risotto, and meats.

Chermoula

It is a North African condiment/sauce that can be used similarly to chimichurri or gremolata. It brightens and adds flavor to many dishes.

Ingredients 12 servings:

- Fat   Extra virgin olive oil ¾ cup.
- Seeds   Coriander seeds ¾ tsp

  Cumin seeds ¾ tsp
- Aromatics   Garlic 2 cloves, large pressed.

  Lemon zest finely grated ¼ tsp.

  Pimenton (smoked paprika) 1 tsp

  Cilantro leaves, and tender stems 1 cup

  Parsley leaves and tender stems 1 cup

  Mint leaves ½ cup.

  Ají Amarillo paste 1 Tbsp

- Seasoning   Kosher salt ½ tsp
- Liquid (acid)   ¼ cup fresh lemon juice.

Procedure:

1. Toast the coriander and cumin seeds in a small skillet until dry, then add them to the skillet and toast until fragrant (2 minutes). Remove from the heat. Cool them down and crush them in a mortar and pestle.

2. Purée the crushed seeds with garlic, oil, lemon zest, lemon juice, paprika, salt and pepper, and ají amarillo paste in a blender and pulse until very smooth.

3. Add cilantro, parsley, and mint leaves and process until well combined and slightly textured.

Note: can be made ahead, placed in a vacuum container, and refrigerated for up to a week.

Creamy Mushroom Steak Sauce

If you find some excellent steaks in the refrigerator, maybe flank steaks (tasty and slightly chewy), you may want to have a sauce to go with them and allow your accompanying complex carbs to absorb the sauce. This richness of umami enhancers highlights the flavor of the beef but also provides for the accompanying complex carbs to step up to a higher savory profile.

Ingredients for eight servings:

1 cup red wine, full-bodied

One cup of beef stock was reduced by half.

Two white anchovies fillets rested in fresh olive oil and then rinsed and mashed with a fork.

Six dried shiitake mushrooms, cut in half.

One shallot cubed small.

1 Tbsp of brandy

Salt and pepper to taste

1 Tbsp of heavy cream, optional.

Procedure:

1. Soak the dried shitake in the beef stock reduction.

2. Prepare the sofrito (aderezo) by sautéing the shallot in 1 Tbsp of butter until shallots are soft. Add the mashed anchovies and cook for a minute or so. Then add the beef broth and mushrooms and cook for a few minutes.

3. Add the wine, brandy, and cream if using. Simmer until the mushrooms are soft. I added salt and pepper to your taste. Add cornstarch slurry (a 1:1 mix of cornstarch and cold water or beef broth) to the desired thickness if necessary.

4. Serve on the meat and complex carbohydrates.

Condiments

Herbs are seasonal. If one desires to have them available during the months outside of the season, one can make herb pastes and freeze them in ice cube trays. Frozen this way, they will keep for months.

Pesto

Pesto is not difficult to make, but often, homemade pesto is overprocessed in a blender to a smooth paste.

Pesto is supposed to be made in a mortar with a pestle, but often, we do not have a mortar big enough to hold all the ingredients. Pulsing the blender instead of pureeing and adding the ingredients sequentially produces a pesto similar to the one made by hand.

If you find some excellent steaks in the refrigerator, maybe flank steaks (tasty and slightly chewy), you may want a sauce to go with them and allow your accompanying complex carbs to absorb the sauce. This richness of umami enhancers highlights the flavor of the beef but also provides for the accompanying complex carbs to step up to a higher savory profile.

Ingredients for 2 cups of Pesto:

- Fat   Extra Virgin Olive oil ¼ cup.

  Grated hard cheese, e.g.,

  Parmesan ½ cup.

- Aromatics and Herbs   Garlic, cloves large, four

peeled Basil leaves 6 cups gently packed.

- Nuts   Pine nuts, raw ½ cup.
- Seasoning   ¼ tsp or to taste.

Procedure:

1. In a food processor, pulse the garlic until roughly chopped (5-6 times).

2. Add half the basil and pulse to roughly chop (5-6 pulses).

3. Add the pine nuts and remaining basil leaves to roughly chop (10-12 pulses)

4. Add the olive oil and cheese and pulse to a rough paste.

Note that it may be refrigerated in a vacuum container to avoid oxidation. If using pesto on pasta. Don't add the cheese to the pesto; add it to the pasta in a bowl and toss to coat with the pesto and the cheese.

Herb Pastes

There is a large variety of herbs; soft leaves are the best for this purpose. Stiff leaves like rosemary or bay leaf are best dried. Any combination of the following is suitable for pastes, and they are stored frozen: parsley, cilantro, oregano, mint, chives, and dill. They are the same in some of the sauces we visited like chimichurri, gremolata, chermoula.

For combination pastes you can use the primary and secondary flavors of the different herbs and use them to accentuate a particular flavor or contrast two or more different flavors.

They can be used in almost any dish, particularly with methods that do not add much flavor to the ingredient, such as steaming vegetables or fish, broths or soups with pasta, sauteing, flavoring rice, quinoa, or pasta, as rubs in chicken or meats before roasting.

The procedure and Ingredients are simple: you need the leaves of the herb, a little extra virgin olive oil, a little garlic if you desire, and seasoning with salt and pepper. If you desire a paste more like pesto add some nuts to the mix. You may replace the olive oil with coconut milk for variety.

As an example:

Cilantro Paste

Ingredients for one cup:

- Cilantro leaves 4 cups packed ± 1 lb. of bundles.

- Garlic, cloves, large 2 peeled.

- Unsweetened coconut milk ½ cup.

- Macadamia nuts, roasted ½ cup.

- Lime or lemon juice ¼ cup.

- Salt to taste.

Procedure:

1. Rinse and dry the cilantro leaves.

2. Place the cilantro leaves, garlic, coconut milk, macadamia nuts, and lemon juice in a food processor.

Process sequentially, not pureeing like in the Pesto recipe. Add salt and pulse once more.

3. Freeze in ice cube trays.

Black Olive Aioli.
Ingredients for four servings:

- 1 extra-large egg yolk.

- 1/2 cup grape-seed oil

- 1/2 cup extra-virgin olive oil

- 2 cloves garlic

- 1/4 cup pitted black oil-cured olives, such as Aceitunas de Botija.

- 1/2 lemon, for juicing

- Pinch of ají amarillo powder

- Kosher salt and freshly ground black pepper.

Ingredients for one ¼ cup.

Procedure:

1. Place the egg yolk in a stainless-steel bowl. Begin whisking in the grape-seed oil drop by drop, as slowly as you can bear. Continue this manner, following with the olive oil, as the mixture thickens. Once the mayonnaise has emulsified, add the remaining oil in a slow, steady stream, whisking all the time. If the mixture gets too thick and is difficult to whisk, add a drop or two of water.

2. Pound the garlic with 1/4 teaspoon salt, mortar, and pestle. Add half the olives and pound to a paste. Roughly chop the remaining olives. Fold the garlic-olive paste and the chopped olives into the mayonnaise. Season with 1/4 teaspoon salt, a squeeze of lemon juice, and the ají amarillo powder. Taste for balance and seasoning. If the aioli seems thick and gloppy, thin it with a bit of water, making it creamier.

3. Serve with crackers, a little toast, slices of zucchini, or garlic slices.

Note: You can flavor the aioli with whatever you prefer, such as herbs, dry mustard, green olives, etc.

Garlic chips

Ingredients: The number of servings will depend on the number of garlic cloves you prepare.

- Garlic cloves

- Whole milk, cold

- Canola oil for deep-frying

Procedure:

Garlic chips are crisp, something you don't normally associate with garlic.

1. Blanching the garlic cloves in milk before frying leaches out some of the pungency and makes them sweeter.

2. Slice the garlic cloves as thin as possible on a Japanese mandolin or vegetable slicer.

3. Put the slices in a small saucepan, cover with the milk, and bring to a boil. Drain the garlic slices in a fine-mesh basket strainer (discard the milk) and rinse under cold water.

4. Return the slices to the pan and repeat the process 3 times, using fresh milk.

5. Pat the garlic slices dry on paper towels. Heat 2 inches of oil to 300°F in a deep saucepan.

6. Add the garlic in batches, without crowding, and fry for 12 to 15 minutes until the bubbles around the chips have subsided (signifying that all the moisture has evaporated) and the chips are a light golden brown.

7. Transfer the garlic chips to paper towels to drain.

8. Store in an airtight container at room temperature for 1 to 2 days.

References

Acurio, G. (2015). *PERU.* Philadelphia: Phaidon Press.

Acurio, G. (2023, July 18). *Comidas Peruanas*. Retrieved from El Mondongo a la Italiana: https://comidasperuanas.com.pe/2023/07/18/el-mondonguito-a-la-italiana-la-receta-peruana-de-gaston-acurio/

Alfaro, D. (2019, 10 28). *The spruce eats*. Retrieved from All About Simmering: https://www.thespruceeats.com/all-about-simmering-995786

Alfaro, D. (2019, 10 28). *The Spruce eats*. Retrieved 06 23, 2021, from https://www.thespruceeats.com: https://www.thespruceeats.com/all-about-simmering-995786

ATKCookbook, S. (n.d.). *The Complete Cooking for Two Cookbook.* Americas Test Kitchen, Kindle Edition.

Benites, R. (n.d.). Estofado de Conejo. *Libro Card-EX Su Receta de Nutricion y Preparacion de Alimentos C60.* Lima, Lima, Perú: Editorial Jurídica S.A.

Benites, R. (n.d.). Lengua Mechada. *Libro Card-EX Su Receta de Nutricion y preparacion de Alimentos Carnes C-42.* Lima, Lima, Perú: Editorial Juridica S.A.

Benites, R. (n.d.). Pierna de Cordero. *Libro Card-Ex Su Receta de Nutricion y Preparacion de Alimentos/ Carnes C30*. Lima, Lima, Perú: Editorial Juridica S.A.

Benites, R. (n.d.). Riñones al Jerez. *Libro Card-EX Su Receta de Nutricion y Preparacion de Alimentos, Carnes C60*. Lima, Lima, Perú: Editorial Jurídica S.A.

Benites, R. (n.d.). Riñones al Jerez. *Libro Card-EX Su Receta de Nutricion y Preparacion de Alimentos C39*. Lima, Lima, Perú: Editorial Jurídica S.A.

Bird, T. (n.d.). *Get Cracking*. Retrieved from Recipes: https://www.eggs.ca/recipes/goat-cheese-souffle-with-figs

Cafe, M. K. (2007). *Mels Kitchen Cafe*. Retrieved from Perfect Chocolate Fondue: https://www.melskitchencafe.com/perfect-chocolate-fondue/

Candace. (n.d.). *The wheatless Kitchen*. Retrieved from Recipes: https://www.thewheatlesskitchen.com/mediterranean-braised-chicken-thighs/

Cattlemen's Beef Board and Cattlemen's Beef Association. (2019). *www.beefitswhatsfordinner.com*. Retrieved from cooking/oven-roasting-basics/oven-roasting-time-guidelines:https://www.beefitswhatsfordinner.com/cooking/oven-roasting-basics/oven-roasting-time-guidelines

Chard, M. (2013, September 27). *Journey Latino America*. Retrieved from Papagaio: https://www.journeylatinamerica.com/travel-inspiration/recipes/margots-seco-de-cordero-peruvian-lamb-stew/

D'Arabian, M. (n.d.). *Recipe of Health*. Retrieved from
Recipe: http://recipeofhealth.com/recipe/fish-piccata-
melissa-darabian-525751rb

Delhindra. (2019, 9 05). *Chef Q!* Retrieved 8 23, 2021, from
https://chefqtrainer.blogspot.com/2019/09/5:
https://chefqtrainer.blogspot.com/2019/09/5-basic-recipes-
of-french-mother-sauces.html *en—Wikipedia org.* (2024,
Jan 8). Retrieved from Wiki/fondue:
https://en.wikipedia.org/wiki/Fondue

Flay, B. (2022, July 13). *Food and Wine.* Retrieved from
Recipes: https://www.foodandwine.com/recipes/skate-
smoked-chile-butter-capers-tarragon-and-tomato-salad

Food.com. (n.d.). Retrieved from recipe-101777:
https://www.food.com/recipe/simmered-chinese-chicken-
101777

Franey, P. (1993, Jan 20). *New York Times.* Retrieved from
Cooking: https://cooking.nytimes.com/recipes/5913-pan-
fried-skirt-steaks-with-shallot-butter

Garten, I. (2022). *Food Network.* Retrieved from Recipes/Ina
Garten/: https://www.foodnetwork.com/recipes/ina-
garten/red-wine-braised-short-ribs-8732915

Get Cracking. (n.d.). *Get Cracking.* Retrieved from Recipes:
https://www.eggs.ca/recipes/basic-souffle

Gore, M. (2023, April 11). *Delish.* Retrieved from Recipes-
Ideas: https://www.delish.com/cooking/recipe-
ideas/a23105767/easy-chicken-fricassee-recipe/

Gritzer, D. (2018, August 29). *Serious eats.* Retrieved from
Beef mains-Italian-stovetop:

https://www.seriouseats.com/hanger-steak-with-bagna-cauda-sauce-recipe

Gritzer, D. (2023, May 15). *Cooking with olive oil.* Retrieved from serious eats: https://www.seriouseats.com/cooking-with-olive-oil-faq-safety-flavor

Gritzer, D. (2023, Feb 17). *Serious Eats.* Retrieved from Recipes: https://www.seriouseats.com/steak-au-poivre

Health Harvard. (n.d.). Retrieved from Diet and weight loss: 5https://www.health.harvard.edu/diet-and-weight-loss/calories-burned-in-30-minutes-for-people-of-three-different-weights

Hill, G. (2022, July 01). *Allrecipes.com.* Retrieved from Recipe/246296: https://www.allrecipes.com/recipe/246296/parisian-style-steak-frites/

Holmberg, M. (2012). *Modern Sauces.* San Francisco: Chronicle Books.

Joann. (2013, March 23). *Fish Piccata.* Retrieved from The Italian Next Door: https://theitaliannextdoor.blogspot.com/2013/03/fish-piccata.html

John, C. (2023, August 15). *All Recipes.* Retrieved from Recipe: https://www.allrecipes.com/recipe/8465165/chef-johns-shrimp-tempura/

KeepVitality.com. (n.d.). *Kep vitality.com.* Retrieved from Home Endocrinology: https://tse2.mm.bing.net/th?id=OIP.NcFuJWQVAtjle0-p6fBSpwHaFc&pid=Api&H=117&W=160

Lata, M. (2019, May 20). *Eating Well*. Retrieved from
    Recipe/273381:
    https://www.eatingwell.com/recipe/273381/grilled-fish-
    with-peperonata/

Laurentiis, G. d. (n.d.). *Food Network*. Retrieved from
    Recipes/Giada-de-Laurentiis:
    https://www.foodnetwork.com/recipes/giada-de-
    laurentiis/chicken-piccata-recipe2-1913809

Lemm, E. (2023, Feb 5). *The Spruce eats*. Retrieved from
    Recipes: https://www.thespruceeats.com/classic-cheese-
    and-leek-souffle-recipe-435735

Lopez Alt., K. (2023, October 31). *Seriouseats.com*.
    Retrieved from https://www.seriouseats.com/ask-the-food-
    lab-how-many-times-can-i-reuse-fry-
    oil#:~:text=So%20while%20oil%20in%20which,only%20
    three%20to%20four%20uses.

Lopez-Alt, J. K. (2017, Feb 8). *Food 52*. Retrieved from
    Recipes/67882: https://food52.com/recipes/67882-j-kenji-
    lopez-alt-s-butter-basted-pan-seared-thick-cut-steaks

Lopez-Alt, J. K. (2018, 08 10). *serious eats*. Retrieved from
    Glazed Pearl onions recipe:
    https://www.seriouseats.com/glazed-pearl-onions

Matherne, K. (2021, September 16). *Easy Family Recipes*.
    Retrieved from Recipes/Ingredient/Pork:
    https://easyfamilyrecipes.com/tuscan-pork-chops/

MayoClinic.org. (n.d.). *Calorie calculator*. Retrieved from
    Mayo clinic.org/healthy-lifestyle/weight-loss:
    https://www.mayoclinic.org/healthy-lifestyle/weight-
    loss/in-depth/calorie-calculator/itt-20402304

Med Stanford. (2020, 01 07). Retrieved from news: 2https://med.stanford.edu/news/all-news/2020/01/human-body-temperature-has-decreased-in-united-states.html

Merano, V. (2018, September 02). *Panlasang Pinoy*. Retrieved from https://panlasangpinoy.com/crawfish-in-coconut-milk-with-spinach/

Morh's, T. (2012, 06). *Cooking Methods Manual*. Retrieved from Web cooking Classes: https://webcookingclasses.com/wp-content/uploads/2012/06/Cooking-Methods-Manual.pdf

Nicole Doster, L. K. (2020, April 17). *A Beginner's Guide to Cedar Plank Grilling*. Retrieved from Taste of Home: https://www.tasteofhome.com/article/a-beginners-guide-to-plank-grilling/

Oliver, J. (n.d.). *Jamie Oliver*. Retrieved from Recoipes/chicken-recipes: https://www.jamieoliver.com/recipes/chicken-recipes/hunter-s-chicken-stew-pollo-alla-cacciatora/

Pacific Seafood. (n.d.). *Pacific Seafood*. Retrieved from Recipes/seafood fondue: https://www.pacificseafood.com/recipes/seafood-fondue/

Pakus. (2019, September 11). *Directo al Paladar*. Retrieved from Recetas-de-carnes: https://www.directoalpaladar.com/recetas-de-carnes-y-aves/solomillo-de-cerdo-guisado-al-aroma-de-la-albahaca-receta

PEACH, I. E. (2021, 04 2021). *Food 52.com*. Retrieved from Recipes: https://food52.com/recipes/22806-eggs-in-spicy-minted-tomato-sauce

Protsiv, M. (2020, 01 07). *Pubmed*. Retrieved from NIH.Gov: https://pubmed.ncbi.nlm.nih.gov/31908267/

Rattray, D. (2023, August 23). *The Spruce Eats*. Retrieved from Ground Beef Recipes: https://www.thespruceeats.com/hamburger-stew-recipe-3057260

Roland, J. (2018). *Butter Love & Cream.* Lousville Kentucky: Four Color Print Group.

Rolek, B. (2022, July 5). *The Spruce Eats*. Retrieved from Pork Mains: https://www.thespruceeats.com/braised-pork-belly-recipe-1135629

Saulnier, L. (1982). *Le Repertoire de La Cuisine.* Staines, Middlesex: Leon Jaeggi & Sons LTD.

Shepherd, J. K. (2017, Feb 23). *Delish.com*. Retrieved from Cooking/recipes-ideas/recipes: https://www.delish.com/cooking/recipe-ideas/recipes/a51691/mongolian-shrimp-broccoli-recipe/

Simon, I. (1963). *The Fondue Bible.* Toronto, Ontario: Robert Rose Inc.

Stella Culinary Chef Jacob's. (n.d.). *Stella Culinary*. Retrieved from Culinary Boot Camp F step curriculum: https://stellaculinary.com/chef-jacobs-culinary-boot-camp-f-step-curriculum

STEPHENS, L. (2021, 04 13). *Food52*. Retrieved from Recipes 22806: https://food52.com/recipes/22806-eggs-in-spicy-minted-tomato-sauce

Stewart, M. (2019, Jan 15). *Martha Stewart Test Kitchen.* Retrieved from Recipes/MeatandPoultry/Porkrecipes:

https://www.marthastewart.com/346878/braised-pork-shoulder

Talbot, A. (2015, April). *Bon Appetit.* Retrieved from Recipes: https://www.bonappetit.com/recipe/slow-roasted-twice-fried-porterhouse-steak

USDA. (2023, 02 10). *Food Safety.gov.* Retrieved from Home/Food Safety Charts: https://www.foodsafety.gov/food-safety-charts/meat-poultry-charts

Wang, C. (1973). Recetas de Arte Culinario Chino. *Chifa Primer Tomo page 68 Receta 84.* San Miguel, Lima, Perú: Self Published.

Wikipedia. (2021, June 23). *Chinese cooking methods.* Retrieved from Wikepedia: Wikipedia, "Chinese cooking methods," accessed date June 23 2021, https://en.wikipedia.org/wiki/Chinese_cooking_techniques

Wild Alaskan Company. (2021, October 6). *Wild Alaskan Company.com/Blog.* Retrieved from Cooking-with-Cedar-Planks-101: https://wildalaskancompany.com/blog/cooking-with-cedar-planks-101

Yanuq. (n.d.). Retrieved from Cocina Peruana: https://www.yanuq.com/buscador.asp?idreceta=434

www.ingramcontent.com/pod-product-compliance
Lightning Source LLC
Chambersburg PA
CBHW042056150726
48005CB00032B/1067